Miracle

ON BOSWELL ROAD

Miracle

ON BOSWELL ROAD

*A collection of short stories about the good,
the gone, and the great God Almighty*

JOHN M. EADES

PROMISE
PRESS
An Imprint of Barbour Publishing

ISBN 1-57748-848-2

Published by Promise Press, an imprint of Barbour Publishing, Inc., P.O. Box 719, Uhrichsville, Ohio 44683
http://www.barbourbooks.com

ⓔⓒⓟⓐ Member of the
Evangelical Christian
Publishers Association

Printed in the United States of America.

Contents

Introduction

Waiting on Halley's Comet, my second book, came as a result of my searching to recapture a sense of spirituality that had been lost somewhere along this road of life as I hurried from place to place seeking happiness. My life had become like the tired joke about the man who was down on his hands and knees crawling around beneath a streetlight when he was approached by a stranger who asked what he was doing. "I'm looking for my wallet," the man said as he glanced up at the stranger. The stranger, trying to be helpful, replied, "I'll help you look for it. Is this where you lost it?" The man down on all fours quickly answered, "Oh, no, I lost it back in the alley." The confused stranger asked, "Then why are you looking for it out here on the street?" The searcher looked up at the stranger and sincerely said, "Because this is where the light is."

Sometimes we searchers are scouring the wrong territory as we seek meaning in our lives. We find ourselves crawling around beneath the seductive streetlight of self-gratification in search of something that will fill up the soul and bring us true joy. The truth is, we have to search in the area where something valuable was lost, even if it means groping in the darkness for extended periods of time. Hopefully, we will emerge tightly gripping our lost spirituality so we don't lose it again.

It has been said that we have three vacuums we need to fill as humans. We have a need for things that only things can fill. For example, clothes, food, shelter, cars, money, and so forth. We also have a need for people and only people can fill that need. This can include parents, spouses, friends, and coworkers, to name a few. Last, but most, we have a God vacuum and only God can fill it up. Perhaps our greatest fallacy is thinking we can fill up our God vacuum with people and things. No matter how many things we possess or how many people are in our lives, these will not fill up the God vacuum and we will be aware that something of great value is missing in our lives. It is no wonder to me that we cannot be spiritually satisfied by money, or sex, or careers, or power, or status, or fame, or any other combination of things and people. I should know; I tried and failed.

As I said, my second book arose from my search for

spirituality. I had no idea that in November of 1996 that spirituality and God would come searching for me. The details of this occurrence are shared with you in the next to the last story in this book and I humbly request you save that story for last. *The Miracle on Boswell Road* was inspired by those events in November.

I have long believed that individuals must have a spiritual transformation in order to have permanent behavior change in their lives. Over time, it has become evident that we cannot break the Ten Commandments and expect to be mentally healthy. Like it or not, we have to return to the basics if we are seeking serenity and peace of mind, and God is the cornerstone of this search. I suppose this doesn't sound very sophisticated, but my dictionary defines that word as meaning "to change from being natural and simple to being artificial and worldly-wise." So I imagine it is acceptable to not be sophisticated in matters of the soul's spirit. God is the centerpiece of everyone's life puzzle, and nothing else can complete the picture for us.

We have too much noise in our world, and we make most of it so that we don't have to be silent. Silence is a dangerous condition, for this is when God comes to speak to us and this means we may need to change. Tolstoy was right when he said, "Everyone thinks about changing the world, but nobody thinks about changing themselves." Television and radio and tapes and games and idle chatter are noisy diversions, but above all they keep us separated from facing ourselves in spiritual silence as God seeks us out for the guidance we need.

The stories in this book were written to entertain, enlighten, and inspire you as you read. They won't change you—that is God's area—but they might motivate you to slow down and examine your life for a while. Even though artistic license has been taken to make some of the stories more readable, all of the central themes are truthful. In stories where names and places needed to be changed to protect the person's anonymity, they were.

These stories are the most spiritual stories I have written and contain many incidents from my own life. Yet, I have faith that these stories will touch your soul. We are all searchers in our lives, and if we only look in the right place, we might just find that for which we long.

An Angel's Dress

"In this life we cannot do great things.
We can only do small things with great love."
MOTHER TERESA

Fannie lived in a run-down trailer surrounded by a lot of broken things. The stove only had one eye that worked, but that was all she needed to heat a can of pork and beans for her lunch and supper meals. The front door wouldn't close tightly and her air conditioner had died during the last August heat wave. It was now December, so she didn't mind that much either. The television was a nightlight but nothing more, and the mattress had springs that sagged like Fannie did when she lay herself down at night.

Fannie had gotten used to being surrounded by broken

things, but it was the broken things inside of her that bothered her the most. She had a broken hip that was slow to heal and arthritic fingers that had forgotten how to work together; but, above all, it was her broken heart that hurt her the most. Her husband of forty-seven years had left her five years ago for a younger woman who had dollar signs—not love—in her eyes. He had made a fool of Fannie and she had paid the price. Yet, it turned out he had made an even bigger fool of himself because his new wife ran around on him more times than a racing car does the track at the Indianapolis 500. It turned out that he had made a major mistake and that he would be paying forever the ultimate price, which was the loss of his childhood sweetheart, Fannie.

Fannie Albritton wasn't a complainer. She kept her feelings to herself and always had a ready smile for the children who lived in the trailer park where she did. It was a rural trailer park and many of the children came from poor families. Perhaps, in a way, it was a city unto itself, where broken things and broken people had been drawn together by fate and circumstances. The middle of December had come and so did Diane Barnes, a nine-year-old neighbor of Fannie's, rattling the loose trailer door as she knocked.

"Come in," yelled Fannie, "it's always open." She laughed at the truth of her words.

"Hello, Miss Fannie," Diane timidly said, opening

the creaky door and entering.

"Well, what do I owe this pleasure to?" Fannie asked, as Diane stood there without moving, looking pretty much like a store doll in ragged clothes.

"Uh, I er, uh, I was just wondering something, Miss Fannie," Diane stuttered.

"Well good Lord, child, get it out before it chokes you," Fannie said.

"Yes, ma'am, Miss Fannie," she replied, then started again. "Miss Fannie, I got selected to be one of the angels in the school play!" The words flew from her mouth.

"My goodness, my precious child, ain't that an honor," Fannie replied, motioning for Diane to come close to her chair. "I sure am proud of you. I suppose they decided to pick real angels this year," Fannie spoke as she smiled. Diane giggled and then became very quiet with her head facing the floor.

"You don't seem so happy, child, what's the matter?" Fannie inquired as she adjusted her glasses and looked intently at Diane.

"Oh, Miss Fannie, I told a lie to my teacher and now I don't know what to do," Diane hesitantly said with a concerned look upon her face.

"What kind of lie?" Fannie questioned.

"A big one," Diane answered in earnest. "The teacher said we had to have silk and lace angel costumes with wings and everything, and I told her my momma could make mine and it'd be no problem. You can't be in the play unless you have an angel outfit." Diane spoke and then fell silent. For a moment it seemed the whole world had stopped moving.

"What did your momma say?" Fannie asked, breaking the silence.

"She said we didn't have money to be throwing away on such foolishness and I should just tell the teacher I didn't want to be an angel in the play. But, Miss Fannie, I do want to be an angel in the play. I want to more than anything in this whole world." Diane began to cry, and Fannie placed her hand on her shoulder and soothed her quiet. Then Miss Fannie rose from her chair and went into her bedroom and returned with a tape measure.

"Come here, precious child, and stand straight for me," Miss Fannie instructed, as she began to take measurements using a stubby pencil to jot them down on the inside cover of an old book lying next to her chair. "You're going to be in that play, child. I've been sewing my whole life."

Diane stood as still as a wooden soldier as Fannie completed her measuring. "Oh, thank you, Miss Fannie," she squealed as Fannie finished, "thank you so very much. I've still got two weeks until the play. Can you really finish it by then?"

"Of course, child. Now run on home. I've got work to do." Fannie shooed her away with her hands.

Diane's smile spread across the whole world as she jumped all the way home. Meanwhile, Fannie alternated between rubbing her arthritic fingers and her head as she pondered how she would ever get the cloth, much less get her hands to hold and push a needle.

Mr. Albritton had left behind a bunch of bad memories and a good tool set. Miss Fannie kept the pliers and sold the rest, using the money for lace and silk. Pointed scissors and pained hands cut the fabric from memory, not using a pattern. Miss Fannie stayed up late into the night, night after night, pushing and pulling the needle, using the pliers to grip it. Miss Fannie also used the pliers to shape the coat hangers into angel wings. Only a person with crippling arthritis could understand the pain Miss Fannie had to endure to complete Diane's angel outfit. All the stitches were tight, and the lace sleeves were the proper finishing touches. It was the most beautiful dress Miss Fannie's frail eyes had ever beheld.

Diane Barnes came by on Friday evening. The costume fit perfectly. "You look like a real angel," Miss Fannie exclaimed, and Diane beamed like the morning sun. "You'll be the hit of the play come Saturday night," Miss Fannie sincerely said. "Who knows, maybe I'll come, if I can get a ride to the school. Now run on home, little angel."

Sometimes going home isn't as good as it sounds. That night a human tornado came into the Barneses' trailer. Its name was "Red" Barnes, and he was drunk and destructive and, seeing the angel costume carefully laid out on the bed, he went berserk, thinking his wife had bought it. His mechanic's hands tore it into greasy pieces as he caused a terror that stopped even Diane's tears from flowing.

Miss Fannie got the word early Saturday morning, and holding a crying Diane, told her to go on to the school that night with her momma and she'd come later to be with her to watch the play. The Christmas pageant was to begin at seven o'clock that night in the school auditorium, and Diane sat in the audience nervously watching the front doors. She was afraid Miss Fannie wouldn't come and that her father would.

At 6:45, an old woman named Fannie Albritton came down the aisle of that country school auditorium with a large box balanced across the top of her walker. She would have been there sooner but couldn't get a ride, so she had walked over two miles before a kindhearted man heading to the play had stopped to give her a lift. Miss Fannie had spent all day cutting and sewing on her old cherished wedding dress. She had used her hands because the pliers were too slow. The pushing and pulling of the needle brought pain to Miss Fannie, but not as great as the pain she had seen in Diane's face earlier that morning. Diane squealed when Miss Fannie opened the box. "Run on and get dressed, child! I came to see the prettiest angel of them all," Miss Fannie said. "I'll be right here watching you."

There isn't any doubt that God was watching that night, also. Surely He must have smiled, knowing that Miss Fannie Albritton would never need an angel outfit herself, seeing as how she already had one.

Willingly

"My command is this:
Love each other as I have loved you."
JOHN 15:12 NIV

~~~

Winona Woodward was a rich widow who did strange things. If she had been poor, they would have called her crazy for sure. She was wealthy, however, and this gave her the privilege of being called eccentric.

"Eccentric Mrs. Woodward" was how the townspeople referred to her, as though eccentric were part of her given name. Someone might say they saw her putting dresses on the fire hydrants that flanked the gates guarding the brick road that led up to her mansion, and the listener would usually respond with, "That eccentric

Mrs. Woodward. Ain't no telling what that old woman might do."

So the day Mrs. Woodward went grocery shopping with Mr. Henson, her butler, chauffeur, and confidant, the manager of the A&P grocery store didn't seem taken back at all when she requested to buy the shopping cart the groceries were placed in after being checked out. There was no haggling over price. Mrs. Woodward never haggled, so the manager became one hundred dollars richer, and she now possessed ownership of a shiny metal shopping cart. Of course, she also left the manager in the possession of just one more "Eccentric Mrs. Woodward" story to tell to his friends.

Mr. Henson dutifully loaded the groceries into the trunk of the Lincoln limousine as Mrs. Woodward stood there proudly holding the handle of her new shopping cart. He wanted to put the cart on the floorboard of the roomy backseat area, but Mrs. Woodward said that was ridiculous. "Whoever heard of chauffeuring a shopping cart on its first trip?" she blurted at Mr. Henson, before ordering him to follow her with the car. So that was the day Mrs. Woodward walked the two miles back to her mansion, pushing the cart in front of her. She held her head high as she pushed her cart along the main road with Mr. Henson following right behind her to protect her from the traffic. The Mountain Brook traffic crept along as though Mrs. Woodward were leading her own personal parade, and the way her mind worked, perhaps she was. The chief of police was out in his cruiser and saw the situation. Anyone else might have spent the night in jail for such absurd behavior, but not Mrs. Woodward. The chief knew she kept a truckload of lawyers on retainer, so he simply passed the line of cars, pulled in front of Mrs. Woodward, and safely escorted her home with his blue light flashing. The chief now became the proud possessor of just one more "Eccentric Mrs. Woodward" story to pass along back at the station house.

Friday came and so did a strange request from Mrs. Woodward. "Mr. Henson, I want you to take this check to the bank and get it cashed for me," she said, handing him a check.

Mr. Henson was pretty much unflappable, but when he saw the amount was for one hundred thousand dollars, he had to ask, "You mean you want this amount in cash, Mrs. Woodward?"

"Henson," she said—she always called him Henson, dropping the Mister when she was perturbed with him— "stop treating me like a doddering old fool and get yourself to the bank."

"Yes, ma'am," he said, as he hurried toward the car.

Mr. Henson returned to find the eccentric Mrs. Woodward had carried one of her many fine dresses out into the side garden, where she was now standing upon it, grinding it with her heels into the fresh dirt as she read the daily paper. The paperboy had seen what she was doing, but beyond having one more Mrs. Woodward tale to take with him, he didn't think much about it; but Mr. Henson did.

"Mrs. Woodward, what are you doing?" he asked with an incredulous expression on his wrinkled face.

"Why, Mr. Henson," she answered as she continued to methodically rub the terribly stained dress into the dirt. "I'm just getting something ready to wear to church."

Sunday morning came and down the stairs came Mrs. Woodward for her morning coffee. Her makeup was off and the stained and tattered dress was on.

"Good morning, Mrs. Woodward," Mr. Henson said as she entered the kitchen and sat down at her coffee.

"Good morning to you, Mr. Henson," she replied. "Please open me a can of tuna and bring it to me." He knew better than to question her requests and brought her the freshly opened can, watching impassively as she poured the juice on her filthy dress. "Nothing like a little perfume to start the day," she laughed.

"Smells like Channel Cat Number 5," his distinguished voice proclaimed as he winked at her.

They left the mansion that morning with one hundred thousand dollars in cash placed in a large, brown paper sack, which was placed in the shopping cart, which was placed in the spacious backseat floorboard; and Mrs. Woodward, who looked exactly like a bag lady, was gently placed in the limousine by a smiling Mr. Henson. Life with her was never boring. Her plan was, in fact, very exciting.

It was a simple idea. Mr. Henson would drive her over to Birmingham and let her out several blocks from a church. She would then push her cart containing the brown paper sack with the money inside up to the front of a church and see if she would be invited in to the worship service. "It's very simple, Mr. Henson," she had told him. "The first church to invite me in will get the hundred thousand dollars to use as they see fit with no strings attached. Any church that would invite me to come inside deserves the money, wouldn't you agree?" she concluded with a gleam in her eye, fanning the tuna smell with her hand as she mocked a southern belle.

Unfortunately, it was not as simple as Mrs. Woodward had envisioned. Months went by and Mrs. Woodward found herself left outside alone in front of pretty churches on Sunday mornings. She might as well have been a leper the way people shied away from her. "Go to the Salvation Army if you want to worship," said one man; "You don't belong here," said another; and one woman told her, "You should be ashamed of yourself."

One Sunday the eccentric Mrs. Woodward stood outside a prominent church and heard a sermon on a speaker system that was set up for overflow crowds. But there was no overflow crowd, just eccentric old Mrs.

Woodward standing on the front steps as she heard the preacher proclaiming the words of Christ:

> *Then the King will say, "For I was hungry and you gave me something to eat, I was thirsty and you gave me something to drink, I was a stranger and you invited me in, I needed clothes and you clothed me, I was sick and you looked after me, I was in prison and you came to visit me.*
>
> *Then the righteous will answer him, 'Lord, when did we see you hungry and feed you, or thirsty and give you something to drink? when did we see you a stranger and invite you in, or needing clothes and clothe you? When did we see you sick or in prison and go to visit you?'*
>
> *The King will reply, 'I tell you the truth, whatever you did for one of the least of these brothers of mine, you did for me' "*

Mrs. Woodward left the church that Sunday knowing why the overflow speaker system would never be necessary.

The summer of 1956 finally came to a close and so did Mrs. Woodward's plan. Despite the concerns of Mr. Henson, one Sunday morning she had decided to push her shopping cart up to the front of the Lawson Avenue First Emmanuel Church in Birmingham, Alabama.

Maybe that was the morning that she proved she was truly eccentric, for why else would she, an elderly white woman, be standing in front of a black church in 1956 in Birmingham, Alabama. That was not all she proved, however. You see, that was the Sunday that the Reverend Obadiah Jackson saw her and personally led her up the cracked cement steps of the church so she could worship her God. All he said to her was, "Come on in, sister, God's been waiting for you."

The Lawson Avenue First Emmanuel Church no longer has cracked steps, or no air conditioning, or cramped Sunday school classrooms. Its kitchen is now larger than the old sanctuary used to be, and that's good, for they serve breakfast, lunch, and supper to all who hunger. They also clothe those who are naked and offer free medical care to those who are sick. They do it because it is the will of God and have the money to do it due to the will of Mrs. Winona Woodward, who, as her last eccentric act, left everything she had to the church that really practiced what it preached.

Rudy's Field of Dreams

"Never tell a young person that something cannot be done.
God may have been waiting for centuries
for somebody ignorant enough of the
impossible to do that very thing."
DR. J. A. HOLMES

Rudy Tucker often was called crazy, but he wasn't really, just slow. On the highway to understanding the world, his mind had made a detour when he was a small child, and it just never came back to the main road. In a way, he didn't care, because the scenery off the beaten path seemed to better appeal to him and the way his mind worked, anyway. He lived alone in a two-room cabin, about fifteen miles from town, and did odd jobs for the local farmers when they needed him. He was country-strong, and when folks needed a human with the strength of a mule, he was the one they called upon.

Life was not glamorous for Rudy, but he got by okay because his neighbors had good hearts and intentions. He couldn't count money, but nobody cheated him, especially Mr. Hargrove at the general store. Rudy would do odd jobs all week and come Saturday he'd walk into town, put his wadded up money on the counter, and ask Mr. Hargrove, "What can I get for this?" Mr. Hargrove would go about getting a food order up, no more than two sacks because he knew Rudy was walking, and always gave Rudy the correct change. Mr. Hargrove took a liking to Rudy, so when Hargrove's uncle died and left him an old red pickup truck, he made a good-hearted mistake. He gave the truck to Rudy.

Rudy put a lot of dents in that old truck, but he kept practicing. Some days he'd drive around and around his cabin until the truck ran out of gas. Then he'd go back to working and walking until he could afford to go and buy some more gas. One day a stranger saw him walking home down Highway 127 carrying a full five-gallon can of gas and stopped to offer Rudy a ride.

"Did you run out of gas?" the man asked. Rudy looked

at him for a moment, then spoke.

"Well, I wouldn't be carrying this can if I hadn't of." The Samaritan knew Rudy wasn't being smart, just slow, so he asked him where his vehicle was stranded.

"Oh, it's at my house. I always run out of gas at my house," Rudy politely answered.

The stranger was a little confused, but he offered Rudy a ride anyway. "Hop in, I'll drive you to your house."

"Thank you, sir," Rudy answered, "but Mr. Hargrove said I shouldn't ride with strangers, so I guess I better say no till I get to know you better." The man looked at Rudy, then smiled, said good-bye, and drove on down the road.

Time passed. Rudy finally figured out how to read the gas gauge and learned to drive to the Starvin' Marvin gas station before he ran out of gas. One night, Rudy put on his best overalls and drove to the Ritz Theater at the downtown square, where he saw the movie *Field of Dreams* starring Kevin Costner. It was a story about a man who built a baseball field in a cornfield in Iowa. "If you build it, they will come" was a line in the movie that stuck in Rudy's head like a tire in mud. At the movie's end, when thousands of cars were shown driving toward the ballpark so far out in the country, he leapt to his feet and began to clap and cheer until the usher had to come and shine his flashlight on him to calm him down.

After that movie, Rudy Tucker was never the same.

He started picking up abandoned bricks and putting them in the bed of his truck and taking them home, where he'd unload them out behind his cabin. He knew where every fireplace was left standing where a house had burned down, and he'd go there and take it down brick by brick, using hammer and chisel, and load it on his truck. He tore down old, abandoned brick walls, and after a while, word got around that Rudy would come get any old brick that anyone didn't want.

One day in the general store some wiseacre said, "That Rudy Tucker was born one brick short and he's still looking," and then he laughed at his own words. Mr. Hargrove didn't think that was funny and told the man so in a direct fashion before staring at him. The offender slunk out of the store. Mr. Hargrove was a deacon and could shame a man just by looking at him.

It was Mr. Hargrove who was the first to wonder where Rudy had been. He hadn't seen him in about two whole weeks. Late one Tuesday afternoon he drove out to Rudy's little place to see if he was all right. Driving up the dirt road, he saw Rudy laying bricks using mud from a wheelbarrow as mortar. He pulled up and tooted his horn, but Rudy was so intent with what he was doing, he didn't even stop. Mr. Hargrove got out of his car and had to walk over and touch Rudy on his shoulder to get his attention.

"Oh, hello, Mr. Hargrove," Rudy said, rubbing his hands on his overalls before extending his right hand.

Mr. Hargrove shook his hand as he asked, "What in the world are you building, Rudy?"

"Oh, I'm building something big! You know what they say, Mr. Hargrove, 'If you build it, they will come'," Rudy enthusiastically replied.

"Where did you get that, Rudy?" Mr. Hargrove asked, rubbing his hands on the rough bricks.

"I saw that movie and that man said it. So it must be so. That's why I'm building it."

"What's the 'it', Rudy; what are you building?" Mr. Hargrove gently asked.

"Well, Mr. Hargrove, one day I was at your store and I heard you tell Mrs. Steele that we needed a new church and maybe, if we got one, more folks would start coming. So I'm building a new church, Mr. Hargrove. If you build it, they will come, you know. Besides, if it was right here, I could come to church all the time and wouldn't never run out of gas."

Mr. Hargrove could only stand there in stunned silence.

"Wait, I have something else to show you!" Rudy cheerfully piped up, then went behind a head-high stack of bricks. When Rudy reappeared, he had a huge cross made of railroad ties and was carrying it across his back. Mr. Hargrove looked at Rudy Tucker as he struggled toward him with the heavy timbers. The setting sun behind Rudy made him a shadow figure as he hurried toward Mr. Hargrove. The innocence of it all overwhelmed Mr. Hargrove, and the scene was one of such beauty that he had to choke back tears.

"That's a mighty fine-looking cross, Rudy," he softly uttered, and Rudy's smile began replacing the fading sun. "Maybe you're right," he continued, "if you build it, they will come. If that's your dream, Rudy, don't give up on it. Maybe someday it will become a reality."

Rudy turned and looked at the crooked half wall he had built and rubbed his hands in glee as the crickets darted through the damp evening grass.

Mr. Hargrove began to tell his customers about Rudy Tucker's dream. At first, they pretty much figured this only proved Rudy was indeed crazy. On Monday, Mr. Ely Sanders, who owned a cement place, said that mud wouldn't hold those bricks together in any kind of wind. Mr. Hargrove agreed, shrugged his shoulders, and said it was a shame that Rudy was too poor to afford mortar for his bricks. Mr. Sanders said maybe the least he could do was tote a few bags up there come Saturday.

On Tuesday, Mr. Morley, a retired construction worker, said you had to lay a good foundation and frame a building if you expected it to look decent. Mr. Hargrove agreed and said it might even be a decent thing for a man with time on his hands to do. Mr. Morley said he had a bunch of lumber and tools lying around doing nothing, so he asked for directions to Rudy's and said he might just drop by there on Saturday.

Wednesday afternoon, Mr. Tyler, a concrete finisher, heard about Rudy when Mr. Hargrove kindly reminded him of what Christ had said about a house built on a bad foundation. "Rudy sure could use an expert's help," Mr. Hargrove said, putting his hands on his hips and staring at Mr. Tyler.

Mr. Tyler exhaled, "Okay, I'll head over there Saturday just to see what that fool's doing."

It was Thursday when a young couple, new in town, heard about Rudy. They said they could help lay brick; and come Friday, seven men from the church figured that maybe God had sent His vision to Rudy because they had been too self-centered and lazy to listen. "Guilt sure is an awful thing," Mr. Hargrove chimed in, and they supposed that Rudy could use some helpers.

Saturday morning a small caravan of cars and trucks wound its way up the dirt road to Rudy's little two-room cabin. The next Saturday, following a story in the small local newspaper, a much larger line of cars and trucks traveled up the same road. Saturday after Saturday, more and more people came to help. Before long the church began to take shape. One after another, good people began to donate materials and money and time and talent. Rudy's laughter could be heard echoing across the wooded hills as he saw his dream start to rise up into the sky.

One day, as the church neared completion, Rudy sidled up beside Mr. Hargrove and said, "Mr. Hargrove, I believe I was wrong."

"Wrong about what?" Mr. Hargrove inquired.

"Well," Rudy softly said, "I always thought if you built it, they would come, but that's not true. I know now if they come, they will build it."

Mr. Hargrove nodded his head in agreement. He saw the reality of the church and realized that it was the result of the faith of a simple man that had inspired the others to become smart enough to follow his lead.

In the fall of the year, the beautiful Tucker Hill Memorial Church opened its doors for worship services. Rudy Tucker was offered the job as full-time custodian, which he shyly accepted.

Rudy still drives that old red pickup around his cabin and laughs as the wind blows his hair through the open window. On Wednesday nights he can be found sitting on the tailgate of his old truck, sipping orange soda as he watches the headlights of the long line of cars making their way up the winding road to the church. Rudy Tucker may never really understand the true significance of what he has done, but Mr. Hargrove is most certain that God does.

found and Lost

Lester McCombs was a fanatic according to those who knew him best. His friends thought it was a nice thing for him to change his ways and join the church, which changed his ways even more. They pretty much figured that his finding God was a sweet event for an old man like Lester, who had lived most of his life with one foot in hell and the other in quicksand. However, they believed that poor old Lester had gone too far in his beliefs. Most of his friends agreed on one thing, that being, that when Lester McCombs found God, he up and lost his mind.

Lester lived in the city in an old house that his father had willed him many years before. It was a huge, rambling house with seventeen rooms that his attorney father had once used for lavish entertainment purposes and to exhibit his status to those "less fortunates" who happened to be his neighbors on the tree-lined avenue. When the house became Lester's, he moved into it and blocked off seven of the rooms to save on the heating and cooling bills. The next day, Lester quit his job at the local hardware store and used his inheritance money, which was considerable, to begin his early retirement and catch up on all the pleasures of life he had been unable to afford. New cars and used women took up much of his time as he made up for his deprivation years by having whatever suited his fancy. Since Lester also fancied gambling and drinking, it seemed his days were just too full to give any real serious thought to where he was heading with his life. Lester never cared if the road to hell was paved with good intentions because, frankly, Lester never had any good intentions in the first place.

When Lester McCombs had his stroke, his partying pals didn't seem much concerned about curtailing Lester's lifestyle of fun and drinking. They sneaked booze into the hospital as he lay there with one side of his face paralyzed. When the alcohol dribbled out one side of his mouth, old Lester laughed right along with them at the dampness of his pajamas. When Lester came home from the hospital, they threw him a drunken welcome home party, and not a person there seemed to realize that they were doing him a disservice. In fact, nobody seemed to care what old Lester did until that fateful Sunday morning he entered the Pineview Church of Simsville and, shortly thereafter, the spirit of God entered Lester. After that Sunday, it seemed that just about everybody started caring what Lester McCombs did with his life.

His old drinking buddies thought Lester was carrying this God thing a little too far and quickly figured the word "hypocrite" was a nice label to tag him with since he withdrew himself from alcohol and wild parties. The folks over at the church were extremely happy to see Lester's conversion, but many of them were in doubt as to his sincerity. Some of those good people even began to accuse him of merely being opportunistic in his actions to avoid the punishment of God. After all, Lester had lived with that one foot in hell for so long that they were afraid he might just be manipulating God in order to not have to pay for his obvious transgressions. They sure didn't care to have the church being used as a leg up for his other foot, if he wasn't going to meet their expectations of him. Listening closely, one perhaps could have picked out a little jealousy and a pinch of paranoia behind their words as they watched this prodigal son returning home. Made no difference to Lester; he had made his peace with God and that was all that mattered to him.

Lester found himself in a strange place once he found God. His old friends didn't want much to do with him and his new friends were wary of what to do with or about him. The truth is, both groups thought Lester had lost his mind.

The preacher was the first person to get an inkling of just how "different" Lester had become since his encounter with the Almighty. The Reverend Bowers had come to visit with Lester and discuss his obligations as a new Christian. Before long, the conversation turned toward money and why tithing would be a good practice for Lester to follow. Lester listened patiently, then announced to the Reverend Bowers that he didn't think ten percent of his money was the right amount to be giving to the church. In fact, Lester told the preacher that he had decided to not give any money at all to the church.

"But, Mr. McCombs," the preacher gasped, "you are wealthy and the Bible instructs us on the tithe and how it is to be part of our Christian duty."

"That's true, Reverend Bowers," Lester answered, "but last night I was reading where Christ told that rich young ruler to give away everything he had and follow Him. I've decided that tomorrow morning I'm going down to the bank and withdraw all my money and head out to Milltown. Once I get there, I'm going to get one of those men that work at the giant sawmill to loan me a table and a chair. I'm going to spend the rest of the day giving away my money to those families that come by and tell me they need it."

The preacher looked at Lester as though he had lost his mind. "Lester, are you sure that's what you want to do with your money? I mean, how do you know it will be spent wisely on things they really need?"

"Oh, I don't care what they do with it," Lester smiled. "After all, it'll be their money and I don't think I'd have the right to tell them what to do with it! I mean, if they want to waste it, then that's their business. My business is to give it and that's all I know!" Lester stood up and offered his hand to shake good-bye.

Reverend Bowers shook Lester's hand that day, and when he got to his car he shook his head. Before long, the rumor mill was doing more work than the sawmill, and by the next day, the folks in Simsville were convinced that poor old Lester McCombs had found God but obviously was on his way to completely losing his mind. The next day, Lester gave away every cent that he had in the bank to the poor sawmill workers at Milltown. Most folks figured that, for sure, Lester was carrying this Christianity thing way too far.

Giving away his money separated Lester even further

from his old friends. They were fair-weather friends anyway, and this God thing had obviously clouded his mind.
Since Lester wasn't picking up the tab anymore, they
simply packed up their friendship and left. His new
friends over at the church felt Lester had purposely tried
to cast them in a bad light by making them look cheap
in their donations to the needy. "Only a grandstanding
fool would do what he did!" they exclaimed to explain
away a generosity that was too frightening to endorse.

That summer Lester dug up his manicured front yard
and planted a huge vegetable garden because he felt that
God would want him feeding the poor instead of win-
ning first prize in the garden club's beautiful lawn contest. This served to substantiate people's opinion that he
had indeed lost his mind. To show how much these neg-
ative comments were affecting him, Lester dug up his
landscaped flower garden in the backyard and planted a
vegetable garden back there, also.

Lester would attend church each Sunday with a
broad smile on his face, and this was taken as one more
sign that he must have received brain damage from the
stroke he had suffered. Why else would he be grinning
so big while church was going on? Nobody else did.

When fall came, Lester got out his hammer and began
to remove the boards from the closed-off rooms in his
house. He spruced up the rooms and got the word out that

he was opening a boardinghouse. Lester had no money now, but he didn't owe anything either, except the monthly utilities. Before the week was out, that old house was full of happy boarders. Rumors got out that Lester was charging rent to the poor people who had come to live there. One of the people at the church confronted him about this one day after church, and Lester confirmed it. Of course, Lester forgot to tell the man that the price for this room and (all you could eat) board was only thirty-five dollars a month!

That winter, Lester sold his Cadillac convertible to a man in Jackson and used the money to buy medicine for his boarders who were sick. It seems one of his boarders had told Lester that his sister had died the year before when she was left with the choice of either buying blood pressure medicine for herself or food for her children and, of course, had chosen to buy the food. His sister had died from a stroke because she was poor. Lester vowed that would not happen in his house, and so the car went as kindness and compassion came to inhabit the old house that some were even beginning to call home.

Lester McCombs was walking to church one Sunday that winter when he had his second stroke. He received indigent care over at the hospital where his father had once been on the board of directors. These days he is back at home and being cared for by those he has cared for and says, "One of these days we'll be heading home to be with

God, where we'll all be living in a *real* mansion!"

But for right now, he is recuperating nicely and excitedly talks to his boarders about what they'll be planting in the garden come spring. Meanwhile, his old friends talk about how sad it was that their old friend Lester had sunk so low that he had to receive free care at the hospital.

Surely, God must chuckle at the gossipers, for He realizes just how high Lester has risen, with the best yet to come. He, like the townspeople, knows that Lester lost his mind when he found Him, and that is exactly the way that God wants it to be.

In the Dumps

*"Blessed are the poor in spirit,
for theirs is the kingdom of heaven."*
MATTHEW 5:3 NIV

W e seem to have some unique expressions for the condition that mental health professionals term depression. "I'm a little bit blue," "I'm emotionally under the weather," "I feel my heart is broken," and "I can't seem to pull myself up by my bootstraps" are just a few of the folk sayings we use to describe that awful set of circumstances where it seems life has lost its zest and meaning. Sometimes, when folks are dispirited and feel empty in their souls, they might say that they are "in the dumps." Well, if we look at this saying for a moment, we perhaps would imagine that it has something to do with feeling like we are used-up, worthless scraps of what we used to be and now find ourselves discarded on the junk heap of life. Charlie Bowers was an expert on this "being in the dumps" business. Why shouldn't he have been? He lived next to the city dump with his mamma and his two younger sisters.

Charlie Bowers was in the third grade and was ten years old. It was easy to see he was bigger than the other children but made smaller grades than they did, having twice failed the second grade. He was also easy to spot out on the playground. He was the tall one with dirty blue jeans and ragged lace-up shoes whose strings were tied in knots to keep them from coming off his feet during the day. Charlie didn't realize how poor his mamma was and why folks seemed to hold that against him. After all, he had nothing to do with his daddy up and leaving for a life of more whiskey and less responsibility; but his playmates teased him as though he did.

Charlie also couldn't seem to help that he had to walk through the garbage dump on his way to school each morning. Charlie's nose had long adapted to the constant smell of rotten food, but the odor lingered in his tee shirt and shoes, and his classmates often would hold their noses and pretend they were choking on the smell of Charlie.

In the early days, Charlie used to fight back with words and fists if necessary. But lately he had found himself in the dumps, and it was as though some unseen force was sitting on his spirit, which no longer soared the way a ten-year-old boy's spirit should soar.

Mrs. Robinson, his teacher, saw him sinking into a silence and decided that she might have a plan to help Charlie get to feeling better. She asked him if he would like to bring his pet to the class for a show-and-tell where he would be the only person presenting. He nodded his head "yes," and the teacher thought perhaps his being the center of attention would boost his spirits and self-worth. It sounded like a decent enough plan, but what Mrs. Robinson didn't know was that Charlie's pet was much different than the ones that most boys and girls kept around their houses.

The day of the presentation, Charlie woke up early and put on his best tee shirt and cleanest blue jeans. The sun was just peeking over the huge mound of garbage in the nearby dump when he made his way over there to find the abandoned birdcage he had carefully hidden behind some old tires. It was still there, and he dusted it off the best he could and then wound an old coat hanger across the broken out bars in the cage to make it secure. Then Charlie walked over to the large mound of newly dumped garbage and quietly sat at the edge of the mound, listening to the rustle of the rats as they foraged for food in the middle of the stinking pile of refuge. Charlie began to make a high-pitched whistling sound, and from beneath the mound of discarded waste came a three-legged rat, which headed straight toward Charlie, squealing loudly as it ran. Charlie put his hands down on the ground, and the rat ran right into them and just sat there sniffing the familiar smell of his hands.

"Hello, Rhonda," Charlie softly whispered. "How would you like to go to school with me today?" he asked, slowly opening the door to the birdcage.

The three-legged Rhonda hesitated not a moment before she put her two good front legs on the entrance to the cage and entered, pulling her one good back leg behind her.

"I'm so happy you want to go!" Charlie said, placing a moldy piece of cheese in the cage for Rhonda to eat. "We're going to have a good time, Rhonda, just you wait and see," Charlie promised, and before long they were off walking through the dump toward the school.

Right before getting to the school yard, Charlie stopped and placed a large piece of newspaper over the cage so nobody could tell what kind of pet he had in the cage. He entered Mrs. Robinson's classroom with a small smile on his face as Rhonda scurried around inside the covered cage.

Mrs. Robinson's plan would have been a good one, no doubt, if Charlie had had a dog or a cat or a bird. But when Charlie pulled the paper off the cage to introduce his classmates to Rhonda, they began to laugh and say nasty things about the three-legged rat. In a few moments it became clear that Mrs. Robinson's plan had backfired, as Charlie stood there in silence among his classmates, who were all teasing him without mercy.

Finally, Mrs. Robinson got the class to quiet down as she banged her ruler on her desk. You could hear a pin drop as she mustered up her composure and said to Charlie, "Charlie, why don't you tell your classmates a little something about your pet, Rhonda?" Mrs. Robinson placed her finger to her lips to shush the class as Charlie looked up from the floor and somehow summoned up the courage to speak.

"This is my pet, Rhonda," he began. "She lives in the dump right next to my house. She has been my friend for three years and is a very courageous rat. She was just a small mouse the first time I ever saw her and that was when she was caught in the mousetrap that my daddy had put behind the refrigerator. My daddy laughed at her, just like y'all did, and when he heard her squealing because her rear leg was caught in the trap, he reached down and snatched her whole body so hard that her leg was ripped from her small body. My daddy walked to the door and threw her into the night, but later on I snuck outside with a flashlight and found her laying on top of some leaves. She was bleeding real bad, so I picked her up and took her to my bedroom and tied a piece of kite string around her leg to make the blood stop."

Mrs. Robinson sat at her desk in amazement as she noticed that the children were being attentive to Charlie's words. Charlie took a deep breath and continued.

"I put her in my dresser drawer and snuck food to her until she was well enough to leave, and then I took her out to the dump so she could join her family. But," Charlie stammered, "she kept coming back to visit me. Before Daddy left my mamma, he sometimes would get red-faced mad and would spank me for no reason and then put me in a closet and lock the door." Charlie's classmates now were listening to every word he spoke. He continued.

"One night I was in the closet and crying, because when my daddy spanked hard, you couldn't help but cry, and I heard this sound in the wall of the closet. The next thing I knew, here came Rhonda and she looked so big and fat I almost didn't recognize her until I saw her rear leg was missing. Every night my daddy would spank me and lock me in the closet, and every night Rhonda would come to visit me. One night she came and had her babies right there in the corner of that closet with me watching the whole thing. I think that was when I first thought that maybe another living thing actually loved me." Charlie cast an admiring look over at Rhonda, who seemed to enjoy her cage.

"Time is about up, Charlie," Mrs. Robinson gently said. "Is there anything else you would like to tell the class before we go to recess?"

"Yes, ma'am, Mrs. Robinson," he answered, then turned back to face the class. "I want all of you to know that I am not stupid!" Charlie's voice was full of emotion. "I know that y'all think I am strong, but I am not. When my daddy left us, I cried even though he was mean to me. I cry when my mamma drinks and forgets to feed my sisters. I cry when you laugh at me or make fun of me. But, Rhonda has never hurt me. She is my best friend, and at night I thank God for sending her to my house. She is a special rat, and you are welcome to come and say hello to her as you go outside to recess."

It is true that Mrs. Robinson's idea hadn't worked out exactly as she had planned for it to, but that was the day that Charlie's classmates learned a lot about what it was like to be "in the dumps." Sure, some of them still teased him, but they were in the minority. Many more of those third graders really wanted to become Charlie's friend, but it seemed their parents thought it best for them to stay away from the dump. When I heard about Charlie Bowers, I realized that the next time I think I'm in the dumps, I will just remember him.

Oh, by the way, Charlie Bowers is now Dr. Charlie Bowers, a compassionate veterinarian who has an office policy of always treating three-legged animals for free, especially rats.

Stars and Such

For as high as the heavens are above the earth,
so great is his love for those who fear him.
PSALM 103:11 NIV

✑

G randdaddy Allen would have been a rock for me
when I was a young boy if he hadn't already become a
mountain instead. He was an unmovable force, and I
clung to him whenever the winds of uncertainty howled
across the tender thoughts lying in the freshly planted
furrows of my mind.

In my eyes, he appeared to be a combination of Christ
and Popeye. He was a spiritual man and a carpenter like
Christ, and his Popeye forearms were huge with great
rivers of veins channeling life's liquids toward his mounds

of muscles. His forearms came from years of hammering nails, while his goodness came from years of hammering out the meanings of God's word as he studied the Bible late into the night.

On weekends, my parents would deliver me to Grandma and Granddaddy's white-framed house so they could be free to pursue those passions that had enslaved them. I always felt delivered in more ways than one when I dashed up the front steps to Granddaddy's house. Granddaddy would pull me up into his massive arms and, as I waved good-bye to the leaving Plymouth sedan, I could feel the tension leaving my body. The world always looked so much clearer and better and safer from that vantage point.

One time I was spending the night with him and Grandma Allen and after Grandma was convinced that I couldn't possibly eat any more supper, he and I walked out into the backyard. Granddaddy knew he had cancer, though I didn't at the time. It may have been destroying his body, but his smile was immune to it and that was what I saw.

It was September and the night was crisp and clear. It seemed a celestial party had been planned for the stars and every last one of them had showed up for the big event. They were everywhere and so beautiful as they danced and smiled at each other in their giant black ballroom. Granddaddy stood there holding my hand as he stared at the sky without saying anything. As a child, I always tried to copy the behavior of the man I most admired, so I stood in silence and stared at the stars just like he did. I looked at his face and there was a slight trace of a smile at the corners of his mouth.

"What are you smiling about, Granddaddy?" I curiously asked, as I felt his calluses on my hand.

"Well, Johnny," he began, "I was just thinking about how big and beautiful this old world is. It just goes on forever. God sure made us a fine place to live in, don't you think?" he asked.

"Yes sir, He sure did," I answered as he held my hand tighter.

"They're starting to send rockets out there," he said, nodding toward the sky, "and someday men might even walk on the moon."

"Really, Granddaddy?" I answered with astonishment. "That sure seems a long, long way to go. Would you like to go there? I mean the moon. Would you, huh, Granddaddy?" I asked.

"Well, Johnny, one of these days I'm going to take a journey to heaven," he exclaimed.

"Where is it, Granddaddy? Can you see heaven from here?" came my childish question.

"Oh, no," he answered, "heaven's on the other side of the stars. It's in a space where rockets can't reach."

"Then how do you know heaven is really there if you

can't see it?" I questioned him.

"You just have to believe, Johnny, and I really believe in heaven," he said, staring off into the sky once again.

"Then I do, too," I quickly said.

He chuckled, then asked, "Johnny, do you believe I carry my pocketknife in my right pocket?"

"Yes, sir, you always do. You said you never let a day pass that you didn't put it right there in your right pocket," I proudly answered.

"Even when you can't see it, you know it's there, don't you, Johnny?" he asked.

"Yes sir, of course, Granddaddy," I answered with all the certainty my young mind contained.

Granddaddy smiled, then spoke. "Well, that's what heaven's all about. You can't see it, but you know it's there because God said it is." I nodded my head. It seemed simple.

Suddenly, I remembered my question about the moon. Granddaddy hadn't answered my question about going to the moon. "Granddaddy, how about the moon, would you like to go there, huh?" I asked him again.

Granddaddy stood there in silence as though he hadn't heard me. I stayed silent just like him, even as I saw a star fall. Finally he spoke. "Well, when I die, Johnny, I think I'm going to stop off at the moon and wait for your grandma's time; then we can travel together, holding hands as we enter into God's precious heaven." He sighed gently. "Now, let's you and me go get another piece of cake, okay?"

"Yes, sir, Granddaddy," I said, and as we turned and started toward the back door, he squeezed my hand even tighter before he ever so slowly let it go.

Most Americans probably can't remember the name of the first man to reach the moon, but I do. His name was Granddaddy Allen.

Cracker Jack

"It is more blessed to give than to receive."
ACTS 20:35 NIV

Miss Edna Blankenship had been around for as long as the neighbors could remember. She had the only brick house in her neighborhood, and if it had not been for her shutters, it would have been the finest-looking house around. Her shutters were painted a bright pink and didn't match the house at all. It didn't matter to her, though. Edna figured since she was in her seventies, she might as well do what she liked. Maybe that was why she took to mowing only one side of her front yard. Seems she thought that her cat needed a good place to play and hide, so it seemed logical enough to her. She lived by herself and seldom had any visitors. If she had, her house would have been easy enough for anyone to find, seeing as how it was *that* brick house, with *those* awful pink shutters, with *that* front yard that had one side sprouting grass and weeds taller than a person's knees. Maybe more people should have dropped by to see her. After all, one day she would become a legend of sorts.

Miss Edna's head may have been elsewhere at times, but her heart was always in the right place, especially when it came to the children in the neighborhood. Maybe that was because she was a child at heart herself. Her momma and daddy rarely let Edna have sweets when she was a young girl, so when she got out on her own, she used her newfound freedom to start buying Cracker Jack. My, how she loved that caramel-covered popcorn and peanuts. Now, in her old age, she loved it even more.

In the afternoons, she would sit on her front porch eating Cracker Jack and, when she was finished, she would smack her lips and smile as she pulled out the tiny cellophane package containing the special prize that was in each box. She loved those prizes, as her eyes twinkled like a new star had just appeared there. Her wrinkled hands would caress each and every one of them. There were secret decoder rings, and little comic books, and little flags, and small whistles, and fake tattoos, and little cars and trucks, and hundreds of other perfect little prizes that she carefully placed in the cigar box with Hav-a-Tampa printed on the top. The cigar box never got totally full, though, because for years she had been mailing the prizes over to the local orphanage as her small way of lifting the spirits of unknown children. However, beginning three years before, Miss Edna decided that come each Christmas, she would take out each little prize and place it in a matchbox. Miss Edna, it turned out, also loved to save matchboxes. Anyway, she would place a prize in a matchbox and then she would place nine of these matchboxes into a square, which she would carefully wrap with a plain piece of white paper. Miss Edna thought maybe it was a good idea that charity begin closer to home, so she carefully printed Merry Christmas on the outside of the paper-wrapped squares; and each December, she'd go from mailbox to mailbox, hand delivering her gifts to the neighborhood children.

There's an old wry saying that "no good deed goes unpunished" and that turned out to be the case for Miss Edna Blankenship. Some of the parents began to gossip and say that the gifts were so cheap that maybe Miss Edna was really trying to insult them. Other parents said the tiny gifts were perhaps a safety hazard since they could easily be swallowed if a child wasn't careful; and some said they would check with their lawyers to see if Miss Edna would be liable. One parent complained that she had found an unstruck match in one of the matchboxes and her darling child could have set himself on fire if she hadn't alertly spotted it. Another parent remarked that there was no way the gifts could be seen in a good light because Miss Edna didn't care enough about the children to use real Christmas wrapping paper and there were never any bows on the small square packages. It was a case of strange irony to see how angry her neighbors had become about Miss Edna's kindness.

The Christmas of 1967 was the last year Miss Edna Blankenship delivered her little gifts to the neighborhood children. Most of the intended gifts never reached the children as indignant parents, who by now had labeled her a crackpot, threw them in the garbage or the fireplace before their children could even open the plain-wrapped squares.

But some of the parents, those who were poor especially, waited for the December visit of Miss Edna and her little presents. She was a special light on those dreary December days as she bundled herself up and, with a shopping bag full of presents in one hand and her wooden cane in the other, began her pilgrimage of kindness and goodness. Miss Edna's heart was old, but it sure was full of love for the young. It may have been broken by the adults, but it found healing in the gleeful smiles of the children, who waited for her as though she were a beardless Santa Claus.

On Christmas Eve of 1967, Miss Edna Blankenship was tired as she made her way back to her brick house with the pink shutters and tall grass on one side of the front yard. Something had told her to travel beyond her neighborhood that day in hopes that her little gifts would be better accepted and appreciated. Her coldness and tiredness had not been able to stop her from making it all the way over to the city housing project, where not a single person had denied her as she gently placed her plain-wrapped presents in each mailbox where children's toys lay on the small front stoops of the apartments like some celestial code that God had given her to indicate where her gifts could best be used.

Maybe going that extra mile had been the final undoing of Miss Edna. On Christmas Eve of 1967, she ate her last box of Cracker Jack, smacked her chapped lips, and laid down with a smile on her face and a secret decoder ring clutched in her wrinkled hand. Later that day, the code to heaven was easily deciphered as Miss Edna Blankenship passed into a land where Cracker Jack boxes never run empty and eternal joy and peace were just a few of the precious prizes she now held in her hands.

Mr. Harvey Williams, an unemployed ditchdigger who lived in the housing project, was touched deeply by the kindness of Miss Edna. His son had received nine little prizes and nine matchboxes, and Mr. Williams was grateful for each one of them as he watched his son's big smile as he played with them on Christmas morning. Mr. Williams was so moved that he even saved the plain wrapping paper, and it was a good thing he did. It seems those indignant parents in the neighborhood who had burned Miss Edna's presents or thrown them in the garbage had gotten just what they deserved.

It was the Christmas of 1967 that Miss Edna Blankenship had decided to wrap all of her little square presents in paper that was plain on the outside but not on the inside, and Mr. Harvey Williams did the right thing when he saved that plain paper wrapping. It turned out to be a stock certificate for the original issue of AT&T stock, and just one of them was worth enough to make a person instantly wealthy.

Each Christmas, Mr. Williams continues the tradition of giving presents to those children who are in need, and he does it in loving memory of a lady who he says was a "crackerjack of a woman."

Not far from Here

*"Don't need no fancy car if yore working for God.
Yore feet will take you as far as He needs you to go."*
MOSES JULY BOGGS

When I was a senior in high school, I went to live full time with Grandma Allen. Granddaddy had passed away several years earlier, and my parents' marriage had died a few months before, following a lengthy period of struggling for survival in the face of a terminal relationship. Grandma opened the door to her house and her heart for me on the day I arrived. She and I were kindred spirits, seeing as how we each had suffered a powerful loss, so I sat my young soul down in her living room right along with my old suitcase. So it began.

The only fashion Grandma Allen had was old. She wore print dresses and lace-up shoes, and I could hear those old-fashioned heavy brogans walking the wooden floors each morning as the sun began to rise. It seemed the very moment I would smell the sizzling bacon and brewing coffee, she'd be banging on my bedroom door. She was more reliable than any alarm clock, and when she yelled, "Rise and shine," I swear that that old door vibrated like a bumblebee. I'd stumble into the kitchen and be seated. I fed my hunger for food while Grandma fed her hunger about me, asking one question after the other about what I thought about most everything that came to her mind. That kitchen linoleum was cold to my feet, but Grandma warmed my heart with her undivided attention. Of course, it also helped that after she had taken the biscuits out of the oven, she left the oven door down to help warm the kitchen with that special blast of aromatic heat.

Some folks might have said that Grandma was plain, and I suppose they would have been right. Grandma Allen never had a wristwatch, she never wore a necklace or earrings, and I don't ever remember smelling any perfume floating through her white-framed house. The only cosmetic she owned was rouge, which she would lightly dab on her cheeks for rare and special occasions. She did use Jergens hand lotion, and that was one of her smells I'm sure I'll always remember. It would be impossible to forget those other odors of Pine Sol, Lysol, bleach, and Octagon soap. My goodness, I hated that Octagon soap. It was strong enough to remove pine tar from your skin, and when you got it in your eyes, it could blind you for mighty near a whole hour, or so it seemed.

The first month I lived at Grandma's, she taught me a lot of new behaviors. She showed me the correct way to make up a bed and instructed me to hang up my towel after a bath so I could reuse it. She taught me how to run the washing machine and pull the clothes through the wringer and showed me where she kept the clothespins. I was smart enough to figure out where the clothesline was located. She explained the iron to me, and when I complained that guys didn't iron, she dryly pointed out that one of those very "guys," namely me, might just be wearing wrinkled blue jeans to school to prove that fact. I quickly got Grandma's point.

I found out lights were to be turned off when leaving a room and the refrigerator door was not to remain open any longer than it took to reach in and take something out of it. "That's not a television, Johnny!" Grandma would sharply remind me when I stood there too long making up my mind what to eat. Ice trays were to be refilled immediately after using the ice cubes, and water spilled walking from the kitchen sink to the freezer was to be mopped up before sitting down. Dishes were to be washed, dried, and put up following any second helpings I might eat after supper was over. Grandma said there would be no "messing and gomming" around her house. To this day, I have no idea what "gomming" means, but back then it sounded like a terrible crime for a person to be committing. After my first month of "basic" training, I became proud of my household chores, especially when Grandma would praise me for doing a good job.

Grandma Allen had a major house rule, and it took me a while to get the hang of it. Each and every Sunday she insisted on my going to church with her. I didn't own any dress clothes, but she showed me to the closet with the mothballs where Granddaddy's old suits were hanging and told me to pick out one. Well, Granddaddy only had two suits, so choosing one wasn't very difficult. One was black and the other was brown. I picked the brown one.

That first Sunday I was quite a sight. The coat was too small and the pants were short, striking my legs above the ankles. I had an old pair of penny loafers and I wore those along with one of Granddaddy's white shirts and a tie. It was the first time in all my life that I had worn a tie, and Grandma had to tie the Windsor knot for me. Despite my outrageous appearance, Grandma smiled and told me how handsome I looked. She put on a dab of rouge and we were off walking to church. The fresh air had diminished the smell of the mothballs by the time we arrived.

That Sunday they had a missionary preaching. He

told of his Christian adventures with the tribes in the Amazon Forest and how it was a far-off place where he had chosen to take the Word of God. It all seemed so heroic to my young mind, and when the service was over, Grandma and I walked home. She moved with a stately grace, while I must have been in a state of grace since no one laughed at my odd-looking clothes. It sure was a relief to get home.

After changing clothes, we ate a sit-down meal, and then we went out onto the screened-in porch to catch the afternoon breeze. We rocked in silence for a while. I suppose Grandma was digesting her food and the words of the missionary.

"You really liked that missionary, didn't you, Johnny?" Her words lightly traveled on the fresh breeze.

"I sure did, Grandma. He was wonderful! Maybe I could do that someday if I got enough schooling. It sure sounded exciting and all. What do you think, Grandma?" I asked her.

She rocked for a time before she thoughtfully answered, "I don't reckon it takes a lot of schooling to understand the soul, Johnny. I think it mainly takes a lot of suffering and a little common sense to recognize that God is the only true healer of hearts."

I nodded my head in agreement, but I didn't truly understand. Grandma must have sensed my confusion, so she continued. "Just how far do you think you have to travel to be a missionary, Johnny?" she asked, leaning backward in her rocker and looking over at me.

"Thousands of miles, Grandma. I mean you got to go where people ain't ever heard about God!" came my answer.

When I said this, Grandma began to laugh out loud. "My stars, Johnny, there's people right around here that haven't heard about God!"

"Really, Grandma?" I questioned.

"Sure," she said. "You could spend your entire life being a missionary right here in east Birmingham!"

"That doesn't sound so exciting, Grandma," I complained. "I mean you've got to go where people are hungry and ignorant and have no idea who God is or what He can do." My young conviction made it seem as if I knew what I was saying. Grandma didn't look convinced.

"Well," she quickly replied, "then you wouldn't have to go very far. Did you notice that run-down house we passed on the way home?"

"You mean the one close to the church with the front porch falling in?" I asked her.

"That's the one," she brightly answered, proud that I had been observant. "That's Mrs. Edwards's place. She's a widow woman with three small children. They need food and clothes and repairs to that old house. That's not far from here, now is it?"

"No, ma'am, it ain't, Grandma," I agreed. We fell quiet

for a moment, then I spoke first. "So you're saying a guy could be a missionary and he wouldn't have to travel very far. Is that it, Grandma?"

"That's exactly what I'm saying," she said with the conviction of wisdom in her voice as she went on. "I suppose God was pleased that we gave an offering to that missionary, but I reckon if Christ had been there, He would have insisted that we all got up after church and marched right over there to Mrs. Edwards's house and we wouldn't have left there until we had repaired that porch and her soul. We would have given her groceries and clothes and a great outpouring of God's love, and it would have taken place not far from here."

I listened to Grandma's words and thought how strange and wonderful it was that there was a lot of missionary work less than a stone's throw from the church.

Grandma stood up to go into the house. "Always remember, Johnny," she told me, "there's always a need you can fill and it's not far from here."

The other night I stood in the church parking lot as Grandma Allen's words came back to me. I felt ashamed that I had forgotten what she had told me so many years ago, and I had forgotten how often Grandma Allen had filled some need for Mrs. Edwards and countless others over the years. I don't have to travel to a distant land, and I don't have to have any special schooling, and I don't have to do anything heroic. All I've got to do is remember that what God is calling me to do is not very far from here. There are hungry people, and homeless people, and hurting people, and heartbroken people so nearby that, if I yelled, they could hear my voice traveling through the night.

As I opened the car door to leave, I felt a soft breeze passing by. I had the strong sense that perhaps Grandma Allen and God were not very far from here.

A New Woman in New Orleans

Therefore, if anyone is in Christ,
he is a new creation;
the old has gone, the new has come!
2 CORINTHIANS 5:17 NIV

Rosalyn Du Pree was as open as the French Quarter in New Orleans on Mardi Gras night. You best not ask her a question unless you were ready for a blunt, straightforward, and honest answer. If you asked her what she used to do for a living, she'd tell you she was a madam at one of New Orleans' most renowned houses of ill repute, although she'd call it exactly what it was. If you asked her why she had lived such a sordid life, she'd tell you it was because it was the best way she knew for a pretty high school dropout like her to become a rich woman. Over her life Rosalyn had indeed become very rich. However, she had been retired for three years, but still, at the age of fifty-seven, she was a most attractive woman.

One night, three years ago, she was leaving her brothel to go to her spacious house in the suburbs when a crowd, which had gathered at the corner, caused her to be curious enough to approach and see what the commotion was all about. There she found roughly thirty people surrounding a Bourbon Street preacher who was loudly proclaiming the gospel of Christ. Most of the onlookers were drunk and seemed amused as if they were merely watching just one more New Orleans street act. The preacher wasn't attempting to be entertaining, but the crowd thought so as they mocked his voice and movements. Yet it didn't deter him from the task at hand as he kept on proclaiming the gospel to the rowdy group while the heavy, humid night air brought beads of sweat to his flushed face.

Rosalyn Du Pree normally would have joined in the festivities and, more likely than not, would have been laughing as she yelled something like, "Give 'em hellfire, preacher man." But this night was not a normal night for her, so she stood there in silence at the fringe of the crowd, listening intently to the words of the street preacher as he wildly waved his arms for emphasis while he spoke. The truth was, Rosalyn Du Pree wouldn't have been listening closely at all this night if she hadn't listened so closely yesterday. Yesterday, she heard every detail her doctor had given her, especially those words concerning her having tested positive for the AIDS virus.

Rosalyn passed through a gap in the crowd as the preacher continued. "Some of you here tonight are drunk, but the day you become drunk with the Holy Spirit you will understand the joy of life. Some of you here are beautiful on the outside, but Christ will make you beautiful on the inside. You may mock me tonight, but there is no way you can mock God. It's never too late to come home. Christ, Himself, has gone before you to prepare a place for you in the presence of His Father. Please, pray with me."

Why, she didn't know, but Rosalyn Du Pree moved closer, bowed her head, and began to pray as the preacher led them in a sinner's prayer while the boisterous crowd began trying to drown out his words with shrill shouts. She sincerely desired to feel beautiful on the inside, the way she did when she was a young girl helping her folks sharecrop a sugarcane farm in the lowlands of Louisiana. She also liked that idea of going home, for she understood the pain of the prodigal son and was weary just like he had been. It was difficult to tell if it was the humidity or tears that started her makeup running down her face, but she didn't care anyway. She left there that night with a permanent beauty on the inside, such being the result of experiencing a true spiritual transformation. That had occurred three years ago.

Rosalyn Du Pree had been mighty busy since that street corner conversion. She had turned her life around, and this turned the heads of many politicians and prominent men who had, well, sort of known her as the notorious madam she once had been. She never would have had to ask them twice for donations to her widespread charity projects, but somehow that seemed too much like blackmail to suit her newfound principles. So, using her accumulated wealth, she went about atoning for her former life by building a home for orphans, establishing halfway houses for alcoholics and the mentally ill, and funding a place called Rosalyn's Restaurant, where the indigent could come and have a meal that was the equivalent of any French restaurant in town. No bologna sandwiches and tomato soup were served there. There were real menus and real waiters. It was shrimp, and steak, and crawfish, and Cajun dishes, and even lobster on some days. It was mighty strange to see broken men and women dressed in ragged clothes sitting down at a table with real silverware, fine china, crystal goblets, cloth napkins, and embroidered tablecloths. Rosalyn loved to see those weary souls having a grand time, but to some of the raised-nose society women in the old New Orleans caste system, it was considered too grand for such losers in life. Rosalyn said it was her restaurant and her money and she'd spend it the way she wanted to.

Well, it wasn't long before some brooding, blue-blooded women began saying that her money was tainted and her charity work couldn't possibly be sanctioned by the Almighty since it was done with money earned in sin. Some of the churches that Rosalyn had made regular donations to came under the mounting social pressure and began to return her contributions with the envelopes unopened.

Rosalyn Du Pree just shrugged it off and used that returned money to start building a recreation center for underprivileged children. She didn't particularly care what people had to say; she got her instructions from a much higher source. Rosalyn was wise enough to know that desperate people desire help, not impeccable family trees from their helpers, so she kept on keeping on despite the mounting criticism.

The experts say that stress and strife are not healthy for individuals with AIDS, and after almost two years her health began to fail. Rosalyn started using a cane to get around and her weight dropped like winter leaves on a windy day. It seemed God was bringing her home one pound at a time.

It was in the fall of the year that Rosalyn Du Pree went to sleep to awake no more. Her funds had become exhausted, right along with her strength, and there was no money left for her funeral. Besides, there wasn't a single church that desired to allow her services to be held within their sacred structures. So many people had cast the first stone that, had there been enough time and labor, perhaps a cathedral could have been constructed for the service.

Rosalyn's body was claimed by a tall, lanky, wild-eyed street preacher named Josh Kendall, who said he came to take his once-lost sister home. The authorities didn't question him very closely, seeing as how they were glad to get her off their hands.

An old customer of Rosalyn's made an anonymous donation that covered the rental fee of St. Dominic's church and bought a simple vault into which she would be placed. The poor people of the streets raised enough money to buy her a burial dress and a coffin made of solid oak. Her musician friends came up with a horse-drawn hearse for the funeral procession and twenty-three jazz players volunteered to lead the procession after the service.

The funeral service was to begin at 11 A.M., but by nine o'clock the church was full. By ten o'clock the twenty wide steps leading up to the church were crammed tight with mourners. By 10:45 the street in front of the church was lined with people standing in respectful silence. At eleven o'clock Josh Kendall wailed his words as he spoke of the woman who had edged her way toward him as he preached on a street corner years before. He spoke of her kindness, and of her love, and of her generosity, and of her faith. Then Ethel Sanders, a beautiful black woman whose head Rosalyn Du Pree had once lifted up from eating out of a garbage can behind a convenience store, lifted her head on her own as she rose to sing "Amazing Grace." Her powerful voice filled the church and flooded out into the streets and rose up into the heavens and caused tears to flow down painted faces with sawdust souls.

Several thousand people marched behind the horse-drawn hearse that day. It was a celebration of the life of Miss Rosalyn Du Pree, and the musicians played all of her favorite tunes. As the huge throng passed through the wrought iron gates of the old cemetery, the musicians began to play "When the Saints Go Marching In." It seemed most appropriate. While the majority of people may have seen her as a sinner, to the lowly street people of New Orleans, she was indeed a saint.

Ain't Nothing but Money

"Sure, Cowboy's going to heaven!
Christ was real big on finding that one lost sheep
and Cowboy's the best sheepdog there ever was."
BEN STARK, 1997

❧

B en Stark had a wrinkled face and a wrinkled life and
nothing he said or did could change the situation. He
couldn't iron away the face that had more lines than a road
map; it was the gift of Mother Nature and the seventy-
two years God had given him. Although Ben Stark would
have liked nothing better than to have smoothed out his

life circumstances, it was impossible to press away those thoughts that balled up in his mind each night. It wasn't Ben's timepiece that had dictated that time had run out on Nancy, his wife. It just was God's timetable that decided last year was when she should be coming home to be with Him. Had it been up to Ben, he would have smashed his watch and made time stand still for himself and Nancy so they could be together forever, but it wasn't to be his choice. So after years of raising a family and more years raising cattle, sheep, and crops, Ben had nothing else to raise but himself up out of the bed each morning. The farm was quiet, but Ben Stark still had Cowboy with him, and that made getting up each morning worth it.

Cowboy was a Border collie that had helped Mr. Stark round up the cows and sheep and always had been a working dog until the day a bull had punctured his right eye with a horn. That had been several years ago and he had sort of "freeloaded" since then, as Mr. Stark was fond of saying. In dog years, Cowboy was even older than Mr. Stark, and they were quite a sight as they walked around the fields each day for their exercise. Mr. Stark had a solid oak walking cane and wore a knee brace on the outside of his pants. Cowboy had a hobble in his stride and a patch over his right eye courtesy of Mr. Stark's fondness for John Wayne in *True Grit*. Sometimes in the evening as the sun was setting, they would stand on a knoll side by side, and from the road, with the sun behind them, they appeared to be healthy shadows admiring God's handiwork. But watching them ease down the hillside, it was plain to see that these two aging creatures had seen their better days.

One morning Mr. Stark went into the den to find Cowboy lying in front of the fireplace, but he didn't move when Mr. Stark called him. Finally, Cowboy tried to get up, but his legs just wouldn't hold him up, and he fell back down onto the floor.

"What's wrong with you, Cowboy?" Ben Stark asked, kneeling down beside his dog.

Cowboy looked at him intently and whimpered low as Mr. Stark ran his hands over the legs of Cowboy who flinched at each gentle touch. Mr. Stark knew something was terribly the matter with the dog he loved so deeply. He knew they best be getting over to the vet as soon as possible, but Mr. Stark was unable to lift Cowboy from the floor. He went into the bedroom and returned with a blanket. He rolled Cowboy over onto it and then dragged the blanket toward the back door. He called the veterinarian, Dr. Sullivan, from the kitchen telephone and told him to be on the lookout for him and Cowboy and that he would need help getting him into the veterinarian's office once they arrived. It took every last bit of strength that Mr. Stark had to lift Cowboy up into the truck, but he would have done it or died trying. Mr. Stark always had been a very determined man. Thirty minutes later they arrived at Dr. Sullivan's office.

Dr. Sullivan did a thorough examination, including x-rays, then came to give Mr. Stark the results. "Mr. Stark," the doctor said, "I'm afraid I have bad news for you." Dr. Sullivan's tone was somber.

"What's he got, Doc, arthritis?" Mr. Stark was hoping. "Shoot, we're both old men, you know. I had that creaking in my joints for quite a spell now. Is that what Cowboy's got?"

"No sir, Mr. Stark, it isn't. It's more serious than that," Dr. Sullivan almost whispered. "I'm afraid that Cowboy has bone cancer," he said, looking down at the floor.

"What can we do?" Mr. Stark asked in a hoarse voice.

"Well, I guess we have several options, Mr. Stark," Dr. Sullivan said.

"What are they?" Mr. Stark wanted to know.

"Well," Dr. Sullivan said, then hesitated, "we could go ahead and put him to sleep if you want to."

"Nope, ain't going to do that!" Mr. Stark firmly replied. "What else can be done?"

"There's a lot of new experimental drugs and chemotherapy as one option and that could be tried along with radiation," Dr. Sullivan answered. "But I have to tell you the truth, Mr. Stark; that kind of treatment is unbelievably expensive. It would be expensive even if he was a human and there was insurance involved. Besides, Cowboy will have a lot of sickness and all of his fur will fall out. If he tries to walk on those legs, they might snap like brittle twigs. Even after treatment, there is only a small chance that he will survive."

Mr. Stark rubbed his brows in thought before he spoke. "Could I take him home and bring him in for treatment? I just can't bear to leave him here. He's all I got and I'm all he's got. If it's okay with you, Dr. Sullivan, I'll plan on bringing him in tomorrow to start this treatment that will at least give him a chance."

"That will be fine, Mr. Stark, but how are you going to be able to manage getting him here and keeping him off his feet while he's at your place?" Dr. Sullivan gently inquired.

"I'll be back in a couple of hours, Doc. Could you give Cowboy something to help his pain and maybe get him some rest while I'm gone?" Mr. Stark asked.

"Sure thing," Dr. Sullivan said with a weak smile.

Ben Stark knew where he was going—to Mr. Haydock's house. Mr. Haydock was a carpenter who had added the den onto Mr. Stark's farmhouse. Mr. Stark explained what he needed. As he talked, he held out his hands to describe the size of Cowboy's measurements, and Mr. Haydock used his ruler to get the dimensions down. In less than two hours, Mr. Stark left Mr. Haydock's with a wheelchair for Cowboy that had four wheels and four leg holes where Cowboy's legs would fit, with his body supporting his weight. It had a handle like a baby carriage and Mr. Haydock built a wooden ramp up which Mr. Stark could push Cowboy and secure him in the bed of his truck. Mr. Stark and Cowboy went back to their farm that afternoon with a piece of that elusive substance called hope.

It was amazing how Mr. Stark took care of Cowboy. He fed him by hand and rubbed his head and scratched his ears. He pulled his mattress into the den, and when bedtime came, he would gently pull the wheelchair over to its side and sleep holding on to Cowboy's collar. Every night he reassured Cowboy that things would work out, and he sent many a prayer up that chimney with the smoke. Maybe they were rising higher than the smoke because Cowboy began to improve.

One day, Mr. Stark and Cowboy were entering Dr. Sullivan's office for a cancer treatment as a woman was coming out. By now Cowboy had lost most of his fur and his eye patch didn't fit anymore but rather rested on his nose beneath his eye. The woman didn't know what to say as Mr. Stark rolled Cowboy up the short sidewalk. Dr. Sullivan's assistant met them on the sidewalk and pushed Cowboy on inside as Mr. Stark removed his hat to speak to the woman.

"Howdy, ma'am. My name's Stark and that was my dog, Cowboy. He's getting well!" he declared to the woman. She stared at him and nodded her head in acknowledgment.

"What's wrong with him?" she asked with thin lips.

"Ma'am, my dog, Cowboy, has the cancer, but he's getting better," he proudly spoke. "He's been having radiation and chemotherapy for months now, and Dr. Sullivan says he's getting better and better. Ain't that something?" he concluded.

"Isn't that awfully expensive?" she inquired. "I mean, I don't think I would spend that much money on just a dog."

Mr. Stark stood there leaning on his oak walking stick and looking to the heavens before he spoke. "Ma'am, that's my dog, Cowboy, and we been partners for a long time. At night, I rub his leg muscles to keep them from shriveling up and in return he has taught me how to pray. I love that dog and if I'd been on the *Titanic*, I would have given him my place in the lifeboat. He's everything to me and that paper stuff I give to Dr. Sullivan ain't nothing but money. It ain't love, and it ain't loyalty, and it ain't company for an old man like me."

"Well, whatever," the woman tersely said, obviously not interested in what he was saying.

Mr. Stark placed his hat back on his head. "Ma'am, I don't mean to be rude, but folks like you only serve to make me love my dog even more than I already do." The woman turned in a huff and walked away.

Two months later, a Border collie named Cowboy and an old man named Ben Stark stood on that knoll up from the farm and watched the sun set. Cowboy trotted down from the hill as they headed home. Even though Cowboy has a clean bill of health, they still sleep together in front of the fireplace, and although Cowboy's fur is growing back, he still gets chilly on cold nights and Mr. Stark thoughtfully builds a fire for him. Faith and love are fine things, and Mr. Stark's prayers still rise higher than the smoke flowing skyward from the old chimney. Why shouldn't they? He has a lot to be thankful for in his life.

Stones into Bread

He who is kind to the poor
lends to the LORD,
and he will reward him for
what he has done.
PROVERBS 19:17 NIV

Ellis Newman was a hard man. Thirty years toiling out in the sun had turned his skin a crusty brown with the thickness of leather. The calluses on his hands were rough and the crow's-feet around his eyes had been earned by facing the sun and life with a smile that sprang from his soul like new corn. Mule farming makes a man hard and mule farming was what Ellis had done all of his life. He had stood in the stream of life until it had rounded off his rough temperament and made his soul as smooth as a river stone. He had known bad times and good and somehow had tenaciously held on to his small farm the way a drowning man does an overhanging branch. He had no interest in keeping up with the Joneses; he just tried to stay one step ahead of the bank. Often, it seemed the bank was a concrete vulture that was patiently circling and waiting for Ellis Newman to give up the struggle and lay down and quit. However, Ellis Newman was no quitter and his wife, Millie, knew that.

Millie Newman was as soft as Ellis was hard. Years of childbearing and child-raising had rounded her into the shape of a new, fluffy cloud. She cooked and cleaned and washed and sewed and was a helpmate in the truest sense of the word. She never complained about her life for she knew that her husband was an uneducated man who was plain-looking and plainspoken, but the truth was she just plain loved the man with whom she had chosen to share her life. She figured that God had made Ellis what he was, and she knew Ellis did the very best he could do, so she had no quarrel with either one of them. She was well aware of Ellis's shortcomings, but when he came in from the fields each day, her heart beat faster at his homecoming. Real love can do that to a person, and she truly and really loved Ellis Newman.

It was the Monday before Thanksgiving in 1973, and Ellis had finished eating a supper of butter beans and corn bread and had pushed himself back from the home-made kitchen table.

"Millie, you sure are a fine cook," he said, pooching his stomach out like a small child. "I feel like a big old gourd that's 'bout to bust wide open." He smiled and patted his stomach.

"Well, don't go busting wide open 'cause I don't care to be cleaning up a real big mess this soon after supper," she grinned, and he winked back at her.

"Say, Millie," Ellis said as he put his elbows on the table, "I was thinking if I could make some extra money, it might be the right thing to do to invite some folks over for Thanksgiving dinner."

Millie exhaled and stared at him. "How do you plan on making any extra money, Ellis, and who in the world do you want to invite here for Thanksgiving?"

"Well, since the kids can't come down for Thanksgiving this year, I figured it would be okay to invite the Beasons over. They done had a real bad crop this year, and I suppose it would be the kind of thing God would approve of, if you did." He searched her face for a sign of approval.

Millie sat there in silence gazing over at Ellis, who

sat there like an expectant child. She reached over and placed her hand on his face before she spoke. "You are a hardheaded man with a soft heart, Ellis Newman, so I reckon I best be saying it's what we'll do. But how on earth are you going to make any extra money?"

"I done got it figured out, Millie," he said with a broad smile. "Those two acres up on the north end got more stones in the ground than that cemetery over in the city. I planned on digging them up and hauling them over to that landscaping place out on the county road. Mr. Sims, the owner, done told me he'll pay me for them."

"How much did he say he'd pay you, Ellis?" she asked.

"Well, we didn't agree on no price or nothing, but I reckon it'll be enough to feed the Beasons!" he proudly answered as Millie quietly wondered how her husband could be so trusting.

"Then perhaps you best be getting some sleep, Ellis," she said. "You'll need to be getting an early start in the morning." She rose and kissed him on the cheek as she began clearing the dishes.

Tuesday morning was cold, but Ellis and his old mule, Samuel, raced the sun to the north field and won. Ellis had brought his wooden wagon with the iron wheels, a pry bar, and some good, strong rope. It was a good thing that Ellis was a hard man, because getting those stones out of the ground and onto that wagon was mighty hard work. He tugged and pushed and hoisted until the sun threatened to outrace them home that evening. Ellis Newman trudged in from the field that day with an empty stomach and a wagon full of large stones. He fed Samuel first, then went in for supper. Exhausted, he awoke the next morning in the same position he had fallen asleep in the night before.

Wednesday morning traffic on the county road had a lot of irate drivers shaking their fingers at the man hauling a wagon full of stones with a large mule named Samuel. Each car that finally passed Ellis was greeted with a smile and a wave from him. He had never owned a car, so he didn't see what all the fuss was about. It was afternoon when Samuel pulled into the gravel parking lot of Mr. Sims's landscaping company. Ellis hitched the wagon and went inside the warm store.

Mr. Sims came out of his office when he saw Ellis enter the store. Ellis stuck out his hand, but Mr. Sims walked right past him and looked through the window at the wagonload of stones.

"Well, there's your stones, Mr. Sims," Ellis brightly said as he faced the back of Mr. Sims. "How much you reckon they're worth?"

Mr. Sims turned around and said, "They ain't worth anything to me. Those stones are too big for me to use. I needed small stones, not large ones."

Ellis didn't know what to say. "Well, if you get me a

sledgehammer I'll break 'em into smaller ones for you right now. You see, Mr. Sims, I need that money for an important reason."

Mr. Sims's words were as cold as the wind. "I don't have the time to be sitting here waiting for you to break those stones up. I tell you what. You take them back home and break them up and bring them back when you're finished and I'll give you twenty dollars for the lot of them."

Ellis Newman stood there shaking his head. "I won't have the time to do that, Mr. Sims; but if you'll give me the money today, I give you my word I'll come back Friday evening with all those stones broken up in small pieces."

"Stones first and money second. No deal!" Mr. Sims sternly said before going into his office and shutting the door.

It seemed the door had also closed on Ellis's idea of feeding the Beasons a Thanksgiving meal. Ellis had no choice but to get back on his old wagon and head home to tell Millie the bad news. He unhitched Samuel and eased out onto the county road as he apologized to Samuel for having to carry such a heavy load all the way back home.

It wasn't long before a long line of cars had formed behind the creeping wagon, and they began to blow their horns as if Ellis could actually make Samuel move any faster. It took a while before all the cars but one were finally able to pass. That one car stayed right behind the wagon and continued to blow its horn insistently until Ellis turned to see the driver was motioning for him to pull over. Ellis pulled over on the side of the road, but the man did not pass, he just pulled over, too. Ellis was afraid that he was going to have words with the driver and, in a way, he was right.

Ellis got down from the wagon as the man opened his car door. "Where you taking those rocks, mister?" the driver of the car asked as he got out.

Ellis couldn't help but laugh despite his predicament. "I'm taking 'em home, I reckon," he responded with a grin. "Tried to sell 'em, but they were too big. Why, what you want to know that for?"

The stranger approached the wagon to take a closer look at the stones. "Mister, I got a sinkhole in my front yard the size of a small pond and I sure could use something like these large rocks to fill it up! How much you asking for them?"

Ellis scratched his head, then asked the man how far he lived from where they were. "Straight ahead about a quarter of a mile," the stranger answered as he felt the large stones.

Ellis thought for a moment, then said, "Tell you what, mister, I'll sell 'em all to you for forty-one dollars and one cent."

The man didn't hesitate even a moment before he told Ellis, "I'll buy them!"

He gave Ellis two twenty-dollar bills, a one-dollar bill, and one penny and told him to follow his car. Before the sun had set, they had unloaded the wagon. Ellis Newman made it to the country store before it closed and bought forty dollars' worth of turkey and trimmings for Millie to prepare for the Beasons.

Ellis had just loaded the groceries onto the wagon when the man who had bought the stones pulled up at the store and got out of his car. Ellis waved at him and smiled as the man started to enter the store but stopped and approached the wagon with a question on his mind.

"Mister, I've been thinking about it ever since we unloaded those rocks. How did you come up with that strange price?" the stranger asked with genuine curiosity on his face.

Ellis smiled and spoke. "Well, when I saw you wanted to buy my stones, I thought of Psalm 41:1 and God's promise, so I figured that was exactly what they ought to cost."

The stranger nodded his head as though he understood, but he really didn't, since he wasn't that familiar with the Scriptures. He wished Ellis a Happy Thanksgiving and waved as the old wagon began its slow journey home.

When the stranger got home, he pulled his Bible from the bookshelf and was amazed at how much dust had collected on it. He opened the Bible and located Psalm 41:1.

He read the Scripture out loud to himself. "Blessed is he that considereth the poor: the Lord will deliver him in time of trouble (KJV)." The man smiled and nodded his head in affirmation. That was the day that two men were blessed by the same Scripture at the same time.

The Giving Back Garden

And do not forget to do good and to share with others,
for with such sacrifices God is pleased.
HEBREWS 13:16 NIV

G randma's house was located right next to a black neighborhood. There was a "pig trail" pathway that ran past the house on the left side, and it was well worn by folks traveling out to Tenth Avenue North to catch the downtown bus. To the left of the trail was a vacant lot in which Granddaddy used to plant corn every year, and left of the cornfield was the black neighborhood. In the summers I got to come and stay at Grandma Allen's. One summer, when I was nine years old, Grandma and I would sit in the front porch rockers each morning after Granddaddy had gone to work. We faced the "pig trail" so Grandma could talk to people as they passed by. Having lived there for thirty years, she knew almost everybody that came by, and conversation would run the gamut from the Bible to the beef sale over at Mr. Bruno's neighborhood grocery.

Grandma wore wire-rimmed spectacles, and she could see people clearly for what they were, just fellow folks trying to get by in a sometimes-harsh world. Grandma's only other eye defect was that she was "color-blind." That diagnosis was made by her neighbors to the right, who just happened to be white.

Two memorable events occurred that summer of 1951. One day about noon the police had brought me home from the local baseball field and told Grandma they were going to put me in the juvenile detention hall if they caught me playing baseball with the black children again. They told her there was a law against that kind of behavior and she should know better.

Grandma was a Cherokee Indian, a tall and stately woman who had God in her heart and no fear in her head. She came down from the front porch that day and, after pulling me around behind her to shield me, told the policemen that they were the ones who should know better.

"God ain't got any laws like that in heaven," she

sternly said. "Kids are supposed to play together. You two are grown men and should be ashamed of yourselves. You have scared my grandson and there is no excuse for that and I'm not going to have it. You are very lucky his granddaddy is at work. If he were here, both of you might be leaving in an ambulance instead of that car you're fixing to get into and go."

Grandma stood there calm as the men began to fidget. The older one apologized and said it wouldn't happen again. It never did.

But that wasn't the thing I remember most about that summer, although it sure scared me. I remember most the giving back garden.

The backyard was big but still smaller than Grandma Allen's heart. That summer Granddaddy Allen got so much work as a carpenter that it was almost dark each day when he came home and went out back to take care of the garden. Grandma said I was growing like a weed, and maybe I was, but I wasn't growing as fast as those rows of corn that kept me from being able to see over the back fence. Anyway, seeing as how Granddaddy was bringing home a lot of money, Grandma decided it would be the proper and right thing to do to share the bounty of the backyard garden with those neighbors who might need it more than we did that summer. One night, after supper, she made herself plain about her plan.

"John," she said to Granddaddy, "you've done made

yourself a whole lot of calluses over the spring and summer, but you've made a whole lot of money, also. I figure I might just leave those Mason jars sitting up there on the shelves this summer. I don't think I'll be needing to can anything this year, so we might as well give away what we can't eat. Does this sit well with you?"

"You mean in addition to the corn in the side yard?" he asked.

"John," she answered him, "you know that's always been the giving back garden." (Every year Granddaddy planted the side yard full of corn to give to anyone who would pick it.) Grandma continued, "I mean the backyard garden, too. Let's make it all a give back garden this year since God has blessed us with so much money this summer."

"You're sure right about that, Effie," he smiled and said. "It's okay with me if you and Johnny will pick it and sack it and be in charge of giving it away." Grandma nodded her acceptance.

That was the summer that Grandma and I picked tomatoes, and okra, and corn, and pole beans, and peppers, and squash. We made up large grocery sacks full of vegetables, which Grandma Allen gave away to anyone who wanted them. She handed them over that side fence next to the "pig trail" with head-on smiles. Grandma seemed so happy to be giving and the recipients seemed even happier to be receiving, especially Miss Ella Mae

Litton, who had nine grandchildren she was raising at her house. She was the matriarch of the black neighborhood, and her word was law when it came to settling disputes between her neighbors. She, like Grandma, wore spectacles and was a tall, stately woman. I loved to listen to them talk. I would look up at them as the sun reflected off their glasses while they exchanged their souls over that wire fence.

Summer began to fade and so did Granddaddy. That fall the garden was gone and the cancer had come and begun to grow. The more it grew, the smaller Granddaddy Allen became, and by October it had whittled him down the way a sharp knife does a piece of balsa wood. His weight fell like the acorns as he now became fragile and thin. Grandma would wrap him in a quilt, and he would sit for hours in his rocker on the front porch slowly rocking and staring off toward the horizon as though he were looking for something he couldn't quite see. School had started back, but I would sit with him on the weekends, and he'd gently hold my hand as he gazed toward the horizon. Sometimes, I thought he was trying to catch a glimpse of God, and maybe he was.

It was a Sunday evening and the moon was bright. It was somewhere around the first of November and Granddaddy had wanted to sit out on the front porch. So, Grandma had put two pairs of wool socks on his feet and wrapped him up in a blanket and a quilt to keep him warm and had helped him out to his rocker. She eased him down and tucked the covers in around his body, then she sat on one side and I sat on the other. I remember that Grandma's face was set with a firm jaw as though she were defying death to ever show itself.

Granddaddy was staring off into the northern sky when Grandma and I heard the commotion of what sounded like a large group of people coming down the street from the left. They neared the streetlight and we turned to see it was Miss Ella Mae Litton followed by a crowd of men and women who began to sing a beautiful spiritual as they started moving toward us. They came right on up into the front yard and crowded around and their voices were as powerful as that moment. Still singing, they one by one began to walk over and place canned goods on the banisters of the front steps. I turned to see that their melodious sounds and kindness had caused a smile to slide across Granddaddy's thin face. They had come to pay their respects to the shriveled old carpenter who would no longer be planting his giving back garden. It was their way of giving back, and when Miss Ella Mae began to sing "Amazing Grace," which was Granddaddy's most favorite hymn, there was no doubt in my mind that God had come to make His sweet presence known. I'm most sure that God was giving Granddaddy Allen a glimpse of better times to come. I also am sure that Granddaddy's staring toward the horizon had not been in vain.

The Yellow Rock

"Sometimes a rock is of more value than a diamond."
DARRIN ROBERTS

It's strange what we sometimes remember. It doesn't have to be the major events in our lives that somehow stick in our brains, like a small animal in a mud hole. Often it is the small, almost forgotten memories that wait patiently for us like obedient dogs to take notice of their existence. So it was for Darrin Roberts the day he found that yellow rock in the attic while he was looking for some lost books that he recalled last being placed there when they moved into the new house. He smiled when he found the lost books and was turning to come back down when he spotted the old yellow rock lying over in the corner. He walked over and picked it up and turned it over in his hands. The paint was chipped, but the words "I love you," painted in red, could still be made out on the medium-sized rock. Darrin had not just picked up a rock, he had picked up a piece of the past that came to his mind, gently tapping on his memory like an old friend at the screen door of his life. He remembered.

Darrin was seven years old the day he found the rock out back by the oak tree near the barn. It was a handsome rock, he thought in his young mind, and he decided to pull it out of its home in the ground. He took it over to the water faucet in the backyard, where he washed the wet soil from its surface and was pleased that the rock was so smooth and round. He would have shown it to his father, Dwayne Roberts, but he was busy working the fields of corn on his tractor and wouldn't be back until the sun had died its daily death. Darrin's mother had left the farm and his father two years ago after she chose the nightlife over the right life. It seemed his father had done nothing but work all the time since her departure, and although Mr. Roberts was still there, it often seemed to Darrin that his mind was elsewhere. So Darrin took the rock into the house to show it off to Grandma Roberts, who had come to live with them following his mother's one-way trip to the city. Grandma Roberts's smile was as broad as her aging body.

"Where did you get that young boulder?" she chuckled

and questioned as she busied herself putting the vegetables in the pots on the stove.

"Out back by the big tree," he answered, as he placed it on the kitchen counter. "It sure is a beauty, ain't it, Grandma?"

"If the county fair had a beautiful rock contest, it would walk away with the blue ribbon for sure!" Grandma Roberts said as she laid the string beans in the boiler. "What do you plan on doing with it now that you have captured it? It's hard to tame a rock, you know!" She laughed again.

"Oh, Grandma, you don't capture a rock," he protested, "and who ever heard of taming a rock?" he added.

"Well, you better let me take a closer look at that rock," she admonished him as she took it over to the kitchen table and sat down. He followed her like a puppy and sat down at the table.

"Yep, it's a wild rock," she said with authority. "You'll have to tame it if you expect to keep it in the house without it running away." She held the beautiful stone in her wrinkled hands and examined it closely with her aging eyes. "I saw a rock like this when I was a tadpole, but I never could capture it. I tried, but I couldn't get it out of the ground. So I reckon you have done a powerful deed just by capturing it. Now, if you want to keep it around here, you best let me tell you how to tame it before it decides to escape."

Darrin loved his grandma. She always could make anything seem mysterious and interesting.

"How do you tame a rock?" Darrin asked with a twinkle in his eye as he played along with her.

"Well, first of all you have to tell it that you love it so it will let you paint it with bright colors. Then you must find pretty colors to give it so it will know that you care. I believe if I were you that I'd get started on that today before it gets homesick for that old hole out back by the oak tree." Grandma tugged down her apron as she rose to go over to the stove. A huge smile covered her face as she heard Darrin telling the rock that he loved it.

That was the day that Darrin found some yellow enamel paint in the equipment shed, and he put it on the rock with soft, smooth strokes until it glowed a bright yellow. The next day when it was dry, he went into his father's bedroom and found a bottle of red fingernail polish that used to be his mother's. For a moment he wondered why his daddy never could tame her, but he was too intent on taming his rock to give it that much thought. That afternoon he printed "I love you" on the side of the rock. When he was finished, he took the rock in to Grandma Roberts for her inspection.

"Look, Grandma, I did it!" he proudly said as he held the rock out to her. She took it in her hands and a serious expression came across her face. "What do you think?" he asked.

She held the rock in one hand as she adjusted her glasses with the other. She turned and turned the rock but still did not speak. Finally, she nodded her head, then placed the rock next to her right ear and laid her finger across her lips to caution Darrin to be quiet. Darrin stood there fighting the urge to ask her what she was doing. Grandma Roberts lowered the rock and kissed it, then handed it back to Darrin, who could hardly contain himself.

"This rock is tamed!" she proclaimed. "It will never leave you. It is yours forever!"

Darrin was so happy he almost cried. He held the rock as tenderly as a new baby. "Why did you put it up to your ear, Grandma?" he asked with wide eyes.

"To see what it had to say, of course," she replied with an earnest voice.

"What did it say, Grandma?" Darrin asked as he played along with her.

Grandma Roberts had a most serious look on her face as though she wasn't really playing at all. "It said it loves you and will never forsake you. It will always be there when you need it and says it would be okay if you let your daddy use it to help him feel happier."

That evening when Mr. Roberts came in from the fields, he received the tamed rock as a gift from his son. His blistered face resembled the rising sun as his appreciation shone down upon his young boy. "I've got plenty of uses for this valuable gift," he assured a smiling Darrin.

Mr. Roberts was true to his word. The beautiful yellow rock was used as a paperweight on Mr. Roberts's desk for the longest time. In the fall and spring, it was used to prop open the back door, allowing the sweet, fresh air to come into the house. One day Darrin and his daddy flew a kite and Mr. Roberts let the string all the way out, then tied the string around the yellow rock as they stood there watching the kite straining to get a closer look at God. One year it was a bookend dutifully holding up the books on the mantel top, and one time his daddy even heated it in the oven, then wrapped it in a towel to place it on his aging knee after a tough day working in the fields. Near the end of Mr. Roberts's life, he would leave his Bible open on the nightstand and place the old yellow rock on top of the pages to mark his place. His daddy sure did love that old yellow rock that had kept its word and never had forsaken Darrin.

Darrin heard the call of his wife from downstairs as he stood there in the attic. As he looked at the rock, he felt a sudden urge to place it next to his ear. He closed his eyes and listened, then faintly nodded his head at the rock. He took the rock and his memories back down with him.

It was a Sunday afternoon when Darrin Roberts pulled up the old dirt road to the abandoned farm where he had grown up. The yellow rock with "I love you" on it was lying there on the front seat of the car. Darrin reached over and picked it up as he got out of the car. He stood there surveying the place where his daddy had spent his entire life. Darrin walked toward the old oak tree in the backyard and gently lay the rock on the ground as he pushed the leaves aside. Even after all the years that had passed, he found the indentation in the ground from which he had "captured" the rock when he was seven years old. He took his hands, cleared out the hole, and placed the rock back from where it had come, then leaned over and gently kissed it before laying his head down with his ear next to the yellow rock. He listened, just like his grandma had those many years before; then smiling, he rose to his feet.

The rock was just like his daddy had been. Always there and true to his word. It was a loyal and good rock and that was the way his daddy had been, a rock that was always there and never had forsaken him. Darrin was glad that he had chosen to grant the rock's last wish. Just like his daddy, the old yellow rock had told him that it had been a good life, but it was now time that he went home.

The Stamp of Approval

In his heart a man plans his course,
but the LORD determines his steps.
PROVERBS 16:9 NIV

Daniel Darby worked for the U.S. Postal Service sorting mail. He had spent most of his life with letters in his hand, and it was no surprise that Christmas was a tough time of the year for the man with failing eyes. He wasn't as fast as he once was, and, being seven months from retirement, his supervisor had decided to dole out some Christmas mercy for Daniel. He called him into his office on the fifteenth of November and informed him that this Christmas season he would be assigned to a desk job handling complaints from disgruntled customers. Daniel had worked at the main branch forever it seemed, and he felt quite sure he could handle the new assignment without a hitch. Daniel began the following Monday and did such a good job that he had several vacant hours left over that afternoon and each afternoon that followed as he idly sat behind his small desk. Daniel suggested to the supervisor that it might be a nice gesture if he could be allowed to use the time to answer the letters that children sent in to Santa Claus by the hundreds. The supervisor grunted an "okay" and so it began.

Daniel Darby was a good man at heart—always had been. His children were up and gone, and he and his wife had even saved up a little gold for their golden years, so life was moving as easy as a barge flowing downstream. He was content not sorting the Christmas mail, and he began to bring the letters to Santa home with him so his wife, Mary, could assist him in answering more of them. Each night they would sit at the dining room table with the letters spread in piles all around them as they wrote brief answers to the children's requests. Daniel had been careful to only bring home those letters that had a return address on them so he could avoid reading letters where replies were impossible. Daniel and Mary would sit and read the earnest, simply stated Christmas wishes of countless children to each other and then scribble off simple replies to the children. Both thought it was such a rewarding activity that they would do it even after Daniel was retired.

One night in mid-December they had cleared away the supper dishes and had just sat down to begin an evening of answering letters. Daniel picked up an envelope and slid the letter opener through the top. Before he pulled the letter out, he clucked his tongue and said, "My eyes are not as sharp as they used to be. This one has no return address."

He started to put it in the wastebasket when Mary said, "Why don't you read it anyway since it's already open. Surely the child won't be asking for more than that little girl's letter from last night. It sounded like she wanted a whole toy factory!" Mary and Daniel chuckled as he slid the letter out of the envelope.

Daniel adjusted his trifocals and began to read out loud:

Dear Santa,
My name is Bobby. I hope you get my letter real
soon 'cause I really need a big favor this Christmas
if you don't mind. My momma and daddy don't
have no jobs no more since the plant closed. We
don't have no lights, but I know you can find our
house 'cause you have Rudolph and are a smart

man. You can see the candles through the window if you look real close. Please try to come to our house first 'cause I heard Momma tell Daddy that there was no more money for food and I heard her cry, Santa.

It makes me sad when Momma cries. I have two baby sisters and I need your help, Santa.

Please bring them some food and some diapers and some money if you can do it. Last night I prayed and asked God to let me come to heaven, so you don't need to bring me nothing this year. The only favor I ask you for is for you to check with God as you fly across the sky to see if He thinks I have been good enough to come live with Him. I know my momma and daddy love me. They just ain't got enough money to feed us all, but God owns everything and I wouldn't be no bother to Him.

I Love You, Santa,
Bobby, age 9

Daniel exhaled slowly as he removed his glasses and laid them on the table. Mary took the letter from his hands and began to read again the words she had just heard, as though the content might possibly change. She finished and looked up to see Daniel staring at the stacks of other letters on the dining room table.

"Daniel," she said to get his attention, "what in the

world are we going to do? We have to find this little boy! How do we go about doing it?"

Daniel shook his head from side to side as he examined the envelope. "Without a return address there's no way to locate him that I know of. It has a local postmark, but that's not much good. He could be anywhere in the city, or maybe the letter was just mailed from here and his family was only passing through the city." Daniel sighed out loud as he stood up from the table. "I don't think I want to read any more letters tonight. I'm going to bed if that's okay with you, Mary."

"Sure," she softly answered, "get you some rest. I'm going to sit up for a little bit and maybe try to answer a few more of these letters."

Daniel's walk to the bedroom had the feel of a man walking death row for his final meeting with destiny. He undressed and crawled into bed and lay there in the dark pondering what could possibly be done about finding this little boy, Bobby. He racked his brain, but there seemed to be no solution near at hand. "I'll call the newspaper in the morning," he whispered in the darkness. Daniel offered a prayer that the boy somehow might be found as his emotional fatigue pulled him down into a fitful sleep.

A touching feature article highlighting Bobby's letter appeared in the Sunday edition of the *News* with the request that "If anyone knows the whereabouts of this family, please contact the *News*."

The Christmas spirit awakened in the community. The excited reporter called Daniel every day to tell him about the amazing response to the article. Numerous telephone calls came in about destitute families in the area. Many of the local service groups like Rotary Club agreed to adopt some of them to ensure that they had a decent Christmas. It seemed like a Christmas miracle. And it was all because of one little boy's heartfelt plea to Santa Claus.

Mary and Daniel waited eagerly for the news that Bobby's family had been found. As the days went by, more and more families were adopted for Christmas. Ironically, the one most desperate family, whose son's plea had ignited the community's giving spirit, could not be found.

Three days before Christmas, Daniel and Mary had begun to despair for Bobby's family. "Why hasn't the family contacted the paper?" Daniel asked.

Mary sat in silence for a moment, then said, "Daniel, maybe they're too poor to be able to buy a paper or maybe they don't know how to read or maybe they're too embarrassed to come forward. I think if we pray hard, real hard, then God will show us the answer."

Daniel nodded in agreement, and they began to pray right there at the dining room table that never had seen a holiday season without food sitting on top of it in abundance. For some reason, sleep came easy that night.

It was almost noon the next day when Daniel received an urgent telephone call from the reporter at the newspaper.

"Daniel, you'll never believe this! It seems a detective with the police department has taken it on himself to investigate all the plants in the area where there have been layoffs recently. He has narrowed the search down to seven families where both the husband and wife worked at the same plant and both were laid off from work in the last several months. . . ."

That night Daniel and Mary, along with the detective and the reporter, got into a van loaded with food, diapers, toys, and thousands of dollars in donations and began driving to each of the addresses on the detective's list.

The boy, Bobby, and his family were not at any of the first six houses they went to that night. While the foursome was grateful that those houses held no destitute families, their spirits began to sag as they headed for the last house on the list. It was almost midnight when the van turned onto Pike Road and began to approach the last address. Daniel was the first to see the candle glowing in the window. "There," he shouted, "that has to be it! The boy mentioned the candles in the window!"

"Calm down," the detective cautioned. "You better let me knock on the door," he instructed. "It's pretty late and they may be afraid to come to the door." He knocked on the weather-beaten door and it seemed a lifetime before a frightened woman and man appeared there.

"Do you have a son named Bobby?" Daniel hopefully asked over the detective's shoulder, then held his breath waiting for one of them to answer.

"I sure do," the man said, rubbing his eyes. "He hasn't done anything wrong, has he?"

"Absolutely not!" the detective said as he began to explain their reason for being there at a most unreasonable hour of the night.

After their explanation, they began to unload the van, and to them it seemed never had the Christmas spirit soared to such heights for the foursome. Bobby was a beautiful child, just like they had surmised all along, and his face was that of an angel for sure as he jumped up and down as though he were about to take flight.

Four tired adults drove home that night, but there was no doubt that they had received God's stamp of approval, which is enough postage to take a person all the way to heaven. Bobby was definitely right in his letter when he had said, "God owns everything." After all, the gifts that were given that night were brought by humans who only had them in the first place due to the grace of God.

The Boy and the Beast

"No man ever stood so straight as when
he stooped to help a crippled child."
MOTTO OVER THE DOORWAYS
OF ALL SHRINE HOSPITALS
FOR CRIPPLED CHILDREN

G ary Woods had never been able to stand on his own two feet. Seeing as how he was five years old and had deformed legs, most folks found that was forgivable, unless they really believed the sins of the father were visited on the offspring. Doris Woods had barely been able to stand on her own two feet, either. She worked at a convenience store and was pinchpenny poor; but like a tough, dazed heavyweight fighter, she refused to go down. Tom Woods, however, had always stood on his own two feet. After taking a few looks at Gary in the hospital, he had gone home, packed, and used his feet to walk away before Doris and Gary Woods had even left the hospital. Somehow that didn't seem so forgivable.

Anyway, Doris and her son, Gary, pushed forward like weeds through concrete. Each day, from 7 A.M. to 3 P.M., she clerked with Gary in one arm, and at night they ate and played. And sometimes Doris would even pray. In truth, she had been abandoned by her husband while, in her imagination, she believed God had done likewise. She figured she must have done something mighty wrong in her life to deserve all the troubles that fell in front of her like palm trees in a hurricane.

Gary cried a lot, what with his emotional and physical pain as his constant companions, and Doris would rub his legs at night until, exhausted, he at last fell to sleep. A lesser person would have cashed in her chips and walked away from life's table, but not Doris. She vowed she would never surrender, at least not on the hand that life had dealt to her. She was brave enough to bluff fate itself.

In the spring of 1992, nature's new life was springing up all around her and gave her hope that maybe she and Gary also had a chance to blossom into something special. One off-day morning, she hoisted Gary up into her arms and walked to the local hospital. The emergency room personnel were nice enough, so they informed her that Gary's condition was not an emergency and she'd have to see a private doctor, preferably an orthopedic surgeon. Doris, who was dangling at the end of her emotional rope, said it was an emergency as far as she was concerned. She couldn't go on watching her son slither along the floor like some wounded animal.

A gray-haired nurse, with a freshly ironed uniform on her body and wrinkles on her face, told her that Dr. Bromfield took cases like Gary's, and she called to make Doris an appointment for the following day. Doris, moved by the kindness and concern of the elderly nurse, began to cry.

"Don't you worry. God will see you through this, my dear," the nurse softly said as her wrinkles rushed into the crevices of her smile.

Dr. John Bromfield walked into the exam room the next day to see Gary and his nervous momma. He definitely was no TV doctor. He was fat, and bald, and wore surgical blues that looked like they had been slept in the night before, and maybe they had, since he was at the hospital so much. His hands were large with long, slender fingers that moved gracefully as they explored Gary's twisted legs. He smiled when he told

Doris his nurse would take some x-rays and then he'd be back to see them.

Doris liked his smile. It was a smile that hinted at a sweet secret behind it, and his eyes twinkled. She had a good feeling about Dr. Bromfield as she waited. Gary returned, and not too long afterward in came Dr. Bromfield. He was direct.

"Worst case of malformed leg bones I've ever seen," he said, holding the x-ray up to the light so Doris could see. "It might take a year or so, but I think we have a chance. It won't be easy. We'd have to break some of the bones and reset them. We'll also probably have to put some pins in several of them. This one here will have to be lengthened and this bone here," he pointed as Doris tried to follow what he was saying, "will have to be shortened. There's a lot of procedures we'll have to do, but I'll give them to you as we go along."

"Will it be painful?" Doris asked with wide eyes.

"Yes, ma'am, it will, but this way he has a chance to grow up normal," Dr. Bromfield reassured her.

Doris glanced at the step stool in front of the examining table and took a deep breath before she asked, "Will it be very expensive?"

"Yes, ma'am, very expensive," he answered, almost apologetically.

"Will the insurance cover it?" she asked in a weak voice.

"I don't know," he honestly replied, "but I do know you'll need quite a bit of money to cover all that's involved after the surgery. You'll need to check with my office staff before you leave. They can check your insurance coverage and give you a ballpark figure."

The office manager told Doris the bad news: "They say it's a pre-existing condition and there is no coverage. I'm sorry."

Doris Woods left the office with the same feeling one might have if they had just met God and then were banished from heaven. Gary never felt so heavy as she trudged back home to their small apartment with him in her arms.

Three days later Doris received what she supposed was a bill from Dr. Bromfield's office. "They don't waste time, do they, Gary?" she said as she opened the envelope. But instead of a bill there was a handwritten note that read:

Dear Mrs. Woods,

The other night when I went home, my youngest son ran to greet me at the door. I couldn't get the thought out of my mind that you deserved to know that feeling. I have decided I will perform the operation on your son at no cost to you. You will still need to raise money for the hospital and related costs, especially rehabilitation services.

Enclosed is a check for $7500 to start the Gary Woods Operation Fund.

Sincerely,

John F. Bromfield, MD

Doris Woods cried first, then she thought. She decided to go to the local newspaper with her plea for financial assistance. The newspaper story was well written and the picture of Gary would have pierced even the coldest of hearts. Weeks went by and money trickled in, but it was not the hoped-for response. Doris needed a flood to cover the expected costs.

Then one day, after a trying day at work, Doris sat down at her kitchen table with the only two pieces of mail she had received that day. One was a flyer for kids' tennis shoes, a cruel irony, Doris thought. The other was an envelope that had Gary's name printed in pencil in large, childlike letters. The return address was the state prison at Thomasville. She opened it and read:

Dear Gary and Mrs. Woods,
We done read about Gary in a paper one of
the inmates got. We figure he done got a bum
rap. We wanted to help. I got no education so I
got no fancey words to say. I been bad my hole
life. I kilt somebody years ago and I ain't never
going to leave this prison. Maybe this money
will help your Gary leave his'n. I must confess,

*Mrs. Woods, that some of the dope dealers in
here was slow coming around but we had a
little talk and they became cheerful givers.
Give Gary a hug for us.*

*Good Luck,
Jerry "The Beast" Bagwell*

*P.S. Get started. We just begun to get the word out.
More will be coming.*

Doris unfolded a cashier's check for $37,000. It was made out to the Gary Woods Operation Fund and signed by the warden of the prison.

And so Gary and Doris Woods and Dr. Bromfield began the work that would someday bring Gary his freedom.

More than four years later, in October of 1996, Jerry "The Beast" Bagwell was executed, and for once in his life has found a peace he had long sought. May God truly have mercy on his soul.

It was in the spring of 1997 that ten-year-old Gary Woods finally ran to meet his mother when she came home from the store. Doris Woods now knows for sure that God did not abandon her. Dr. Bromfield is still not a TV doctor, but then guardian angels aren't much for publicity anyway.

The Room

A unt Grace was a strange woman. She and Uncle Mose ran a mom-and-pop grocery store and gas station in a small town about thirty miles up from Birmingham. In her younger days she had been a nurse at Dr. Walker's office, working for him for twenty-five years. Dr. Walker was one of those old-time doctors. He smoked too many cigarettes, drank too much coffee, and made too many house calls. Then one day, it was as though his heart had beat too many times and it just quit on him. After that, Aunt Grace quit nursing because she didn't want to start over with a new doctor. She and Uncle Mose sank all their money into that little store along the two-lane blacktop road.

The small town where they lived was known for its coal mines. It was a town of hard men and hard times. On Friday nights, men came to her store to wrap callused hands around soothing cold beers. On Saturday mornings, women with worried faces came to buy groceries—usually on credit. Most everybody knew Aunt Grace and called her Aunt Grace, just like I did, except they were grown-ups and I was only seven years old.

There was a room at the back of the store that only had one key to it and Aunt Grace was the one with that key. Sometimes I'd see her go into that secret room with customers who came into the store. Usually the customers would have real serious looks on their faces, and I figured whatever was going on back there was none of my business. At least that's what Aunt Grace told me, and I felt she meant business, so I never dared ask. One day I did overhear Uncle Mose telling her that what she was doing was against the law, but she just shook her finger at him and stared until he couldn't take her look any longer and went outside to pump gas. Uncle Mose was a tough old man, but Aunt Grace always was able to intimidate him. In fact, if I didn't know how sweet she was, I'd have thought she was like a godfather, or godmother, that is, in the Mafia. Her word was the law, and I remember one time she even took the sheriff into her secret room. He was smiling real big when they came out, with his hat in his hand, of course.

We moved away—Daddy had found a better job—and every now and then we'd get a Christmas card from Aunt Grace. When I was twenty, my grandma got word that Aunt Grace's heart, just like Dr. Walker's, had quit beating early one Saturday morning. I was in Florida playing baseball and didn't go to the funeral.

Fall came, bringing its usual nostalgia, and I found myself riding out from Birmingham to see where she was laid to rest. She had been buried in the small church cemetery about three miles from the old store. I found her grave site and couldn't believe the amount of flowers surrounding her grave. Uncle Mose had had her favorite poem engraved on her headstone, and I stood there reading it as the leaves fell softly. It read:

Do not stand at my grave and weep,
I am not there, I do not sleep,
I am a thousand winds that blow,
I am the diamond glint upon the snow,
I am the sunshine on ripened grain,
I am the gentle autumn rain,
When you awake in the morning hush,
I am the swift, uplifting rush
of speckled birds in circled flight,
I am the silent star that shines at night,

Do not stand at my grave and cry,
I am not there. I did not die.

I was so intent on reading the words that I didn't see Jacob, the caretaker of the cemetery, until I heard the leaves crackling right next to me. I knew it was Jacob because Aunt Grace had introduced him to me when I was a child and told me he was a giant. He was still a giant.

"We have a lot of visitors to this grave," he said in a deep, reverent voice. "Are you family or friend, young man?" he inquired, not remembering me as I did him.

"She was my aunt," I answered in a soft tone. "I don't believe I've ever seen so many flowers. Did something special just take place?"

Jacob smiled. "Oh, my, nothing special," he said. "That's just the way it always is."

"What do you mean?" I asked, still not certain what he was meaning.

"Well," Jacob began to explain, "ain't hardly a day goes by that somebody don't come here and put flowers down. Yore Aunt Grace touched a lot of lives, son. Some folks come here every week, just like clockwork. I reckon she might have been one of those angels in disguise I've heard told about. I reckon God done let her live right here on this earth for a spell. God knows that favorite poem of hers is the gospel truth. She lives on in the minds of most everybody in these parts." Jacob pointed his huge finger toward his temple to emphasize his words.

Suddenly I felt very ashamed that I hadn't brought some flowers. Jacob must have sensed my embarrassment and quickly made conversation. "What do you remember most about yore Aunt Grace?" he asked with a genuine interest and a smile.

"Well, she was mighty sweet to me," I wistfully answered, "always giving me candy when I was a small boy and really listening to me when I talked. And the way she looked at me. It was like she could see all the way through my head. One time I asked her about that back room and she gave me that look, if you know what I mean."

"I sure do," Jacob said, chuckling in remembrance. "Hey, are you that little boy, Johnny, that I met one summer at Aunt Grace's store?"

"I sure am," I answered. "Jacob," I said, "what was in that back room? I never did know."

Jacob stood in silence for a moment, then spoke. "Well, yore Aunt Grace is gone now, so I guess there's no harm in telling you. You see, for twenty years, son, yore Aunt Grace doctored just 'bout everybody in this town. We didn't have any doctors up this way, and most folks couldn't get to Birmingham even if they had the money to go to a doctor, which most of them didn't. That back room was her medical office, and she had everything in the world back there from doctoring medicines to leg braces. I bet you she sewed more stitches than those women over at the glove factory. I guess the truth was she was practicing medicine without the proper license. Course, it was the town's secret, too, so no one ever told the authorities. I guess what she done was illegal, but it sure meant a lot to the poor folks in this little town."

I thanked Jacob for sharing the community's secret with me. Silently, I marveled at Aunt Grace sharing her life with so many grateful people. I suppose she had the greatest room right there in her heart, and that was no secret, since most everyone had a key to it.

Natural Born Loser

"Let your light shine before men,
that they may see your good deeds
and praise your Father in heaven."
MATTHEW 5:16 NIV

M r. Maurice Rice was Matt Rice's father, and Matt and I played Little League baseball together when we were just puppies. Matt was a good boy but a bad baseball player, yet he had a great attitude, especially for someone who rarely got to play. He'd sit on the bench and yell for our team as though his very life were being threatened. He encouraged his fellow players who might have been having an off day, and never once did I hear him criticize anybody—not his team, or the opposing team, or even the umpires, despite the fact we thought this might make us look exceedingly wise and grown-up if we did.

As time went by, Matt still played sports, but school was what sang to his soul. Matthew Rice went on to become a neurosurgeon and could probably buy his own baseball team if he wanted to spend his money on some guys who might have a hard time spelling what he had become. No doubt about it, if I ever go to a high school reunion, he'll be the first man I'll be looking up when I enter through the door. His father, Mr. Maurice Rice, sure did a fine job of raising him; and looking back on it, he had a powerful influence on my life also.

Mr. Rice was a veteran of World War II, and I remember he was quiet with steel blue eyes and a crew cut. He spoke as if God had put a limit on the number of words he could speak in his lifetime and he wasn't going to waste even one of them. Since he seldom spoke, I always paid close attention whenever he did, and I noticed the adults did, too. He was definitely a man of few words; and I'm positive that in his later years, when he most assuredly went on to heaven, he had a whole bunch of unused words that he turned back in to God.

I remember one night we were playing baseball in

another city and the crowd was plenty rough on us, as if the adults had forgotten we were only eleven years old that summer. There was this huge man standing right behind the backstop, and every time I threw a pitch, he would throw an insult back at me. I saw Mr. Rice come down from the stands and edge right up next to him. In a few seconds the man left the stadium and didn't come back. I didn't know it then, but later I heard my daddy tell my momma that Mr. Rice had simply told the man: "Leave walking or leave stretched out." My daddy voiced his conviction that the abusive man had made a very wise choice.

It sure was comforting to know Mr. Rice was on your side. It gave me a real safe feeling when he was around. When he would treat us to hotdogs after the game, I thought maybe I knew how it felt to be Matt, as Mr. Rice stood there with his smile doing his talking for him. No wonder Matt would rather go home after school than hang around the park with us. His daddy was really a special man, even though he was what you would call a natural born loser.

It's hard to explain how I could have ever seen him as a natural born loser. Maybe I was just a dumb kid, or perhaps naive would be the better word. I can't truly recall the very first time I got the idea that Mr. Rice may have had a tendency to lose things, but it seems it was that time I needed a new pair of baseball shoes. Being a pitcher, I had worn out the toe of my right shoe by pushing off the pitcher's mound and dragging it across the dirt of the mound each time I threw a pitch. I'm sure my momma would have bought me a pair if she could've, but the truth was we just didn't have the extra money, especially since Daddy had begun to make more frequent stops at the tavern on his way home from work. I do remember standing beside Mr. Rice's station wagon that day when he placed his right hand on his hip pocket as a cloudy, worried look crept across his usual sunny face.

"What's wrong, Mr. Rice?" I asked him, not believing that such an intelligent man like him could possibly lose his wallet.

"I seem to have lost my billfold," he answered, checking all of his pockets as he leaned over and peered into the front seat of the station wagon. "There was a lot of money in it; I have to find it. I'll go tell the other boys to start looking for it. I'll give a twenty-dollar reward to whoever finds it," he announced as he started over toward the ball diamond with me right behind him like I was a big imprinted duckling. Suddenly he stopped and turned around and instructed me to stay right where I was. "You stay here and check around on the inside of the station wagon. Maybe it fell under the seat."

I went and opened the driver's door and bent down, running my hand beneath the seat as I searched for his wallet. My hand came to rest on his thick leather billfold, and I clearly recall hitting my head on the door frame as I raised up quickly to yell that I had found it.

Mr. Rice came back to the car, shook my hand, and thanked me for the good deed I had done. He opened his wallet and pulled out a crisp, new twenty-dollar bill and handed it to me. "Well, Johnny," he said, "what are you going to spend your reward on?"

I glanced down at my white-socked toe sticking out of my right baseball shoe and quickly smiled. "I sorta thought I'd get me a new pair of baseball shoes, Mr. Rice, but I feel funny about taking the reward money. I think I'd feel better if you let me give it back to you. I didn't do nothing to earn this much." I held the twenty-dollar bill in my hand and pushed it out toward him.

Mr. Rice closed my hand over the bill with his hand as he smiled. "You saved me hundreds of dollars and that's the end of the matter. After practice I'll take you over to Dixie Sporting Goods to be sure you don't spend it on a bunch of foolishness instead of shoes."

That was how Mr. Rice's pattern of losing stuff began, and I guess I almost felt sorry for him in a way, like he was some kind of absentminded old man who at times needed looking after.

I'm not sure exactly how much stuff he lost when I was growing up, but it seems it was quite a bit as I think back on it. He must have lost his wallet at least a dozen times, and I suppose I became an expert at finding it for him. Of course, he always gave me a reward. I imagine I was the luckiest boy in East Birmingham, and I never once saw the need for a four-leaf clover.

One time I found a brand-new baseball just lying in my front yard on a Sunday morning when Momma and I got home from church. Several times I found a lot of change in the front yard and most all of the coins were fifty-cent pieces. One time at the Little League field I found a shirt that looked brand-new and it was mighty lucky that it happened to be my exact size. One time the mailman brought my momma an anonymous letter addressed to "Youngest Occupant" and it turned out that it contained a free ticket to a Birmingham Barons home game, which luckily Matt and his daddy were going to that very night, so I had a free ride. Of course that was the night that Mr. Rice lost his car keys in the parking lot of old Rickwood Stadium as we were walking toward the car after the game. We were starting to wonder how in the world we were going to get home. If I hadn't spotted them nestled down in the cuff of one of his pant legs, we could have been there all night. Why, he was so grateful that he let me steer that big old station wagon around the empty parking lot that summer night, plus he bought me two hotdogs to take home with me. I was lucky that they were selling them for half price since the game was over. That's why I got two instead of one, or at least that's what Mr. Rice had said.

I reckon I could tell you more about Mr. Maurice

Rice, but I'm sure you have the picture in focus by now. If ever a natural born loser was born, he was the one, and they broke the mold after him. Sometimes, late at night when it is quiet and everyone is in bed, I think back over my life and realize how selfish I have been in the living of my years. Those nights I go to bed and in the stillness pray to God that He will make me a natural born loser, exactly like Mr. Maurice Rice.

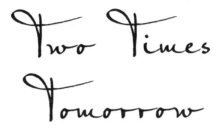

Two Times Tomorrow

He heals the brokenhearted and binds up their wounds.
PSALM 147:3 NIV

It had finally come down to this. Mr. Watkins sat at the cluttered kitchen table as he twisted the handle on the manual can opener to open his and Larry's last can of food. It was Larry's favorite and old Mr. Watkins couldn't help but smile seeing as he knew how hungry Larry was. Mr. Watkins took a tablespoon and gave Larry the first bite before he took one himself. It was quite a sight watching Mr. Watkins and his dog, Larry, eating from the same can of dog food. Soon the can was empty and the old man scraped his arthritic fingers around the inside of the can to give the last little bit to Larry, who sat there licking his master's hand. Convinced it was all gone, Mr. Watkins petted Larry and suggested they go try to get some sleep before their hunger pangs caught up with them again.

It was late November in Birmingham and winter had come early. The utilities people thought Mr. Watkins had utilized their services long enough without payment, so their decision had been to cut them off, proving coldness is never limited to just the weather. Still, once Mr. Watkins and Larry had snuggled beneath the heavy quilt, their bodies produced enough heat to keep them both warm until morning, when once again their stomachs would remind them of their plight in life. Mr. Watkins held Larry in his arms and stroked his head. They had been together for fifteen years and had never, not once, been out of each other's sight in all that time. When Mrs. Watkins went home to be with God, it seemed He had sent Larry to be found by Mr. Watkins that Sunday morning over in the parking lot of the A&P grocery store.

Mr. Watkins pulled the covers up around Larry's ears. "Listen, Larry," the old man whispered, "tomorrow is going to be a better day, you just wait and see. Why, it's going to be so good that it will be a two times tomorrow day. You just wait and see. I've got a feeling in my bones that something good will happen and we'll be eating steaks before sundown." His old dog whined and exhaled before settling in for a night of dreams of chasing rabbits and rubber balls. Morning and hunger came much too quickly.

Mr. Watkins put the leash on Larry, and they were out on the pavement before the morning work traffic had begun. Mr. Watkins was a desperate man that morning as he made his way toward the A&P grocery store. They didn't particularly want him to come in their store anymore following that time they tried to have him arrested for stealing dog food so that he and Larry could eat to calm the storm in their stomachs. But this time was different. This time Mr. Watkins had a twenty-two pistol in the right pocket of his worn and wrinkled overcoat. Maybe the old country song was right when it said "Anything goes when everything is gone." It was all gone this morning, and Mr. Watkins had made up his mind to take that two times tomorrow goodness by force. He tied Larry to the post outside and entered the A&P with hunger and fear.

Mr. Watkins got a shopping cart and went up and down every aisle in that A&P grocery store. He filled the basket with steaks and hamburger and cheese and loaded it to the top with Larry's favorite dog food. He finished by getting some chew toys and rawhide bones, then he made his way toward the cash register. A heavyset clerk with red lipstick began pulling the groceries across the automatic price scanner. The rawhide bones were the last items she rang up.

"That'll be $173.57," she said as she began loading the groceries into plastic bags.

Mr. Watkins felt his hand position the pistol in his pocket as she paused her sacking and waited for him to pay. He could not do it. The pistol simply wouldn't budge.

"I'm sorry, but I seem to have left my checkbook at home," Mr. Watkins apologized to the impatient lady as she exhaled her anger through her nose like an enraged bull.

"I'll just save it till you get back with your money then!" she fumed, mumbling something about absent-minded old fools beneath her breath as he shrugged his shoulders and left the store.

Larry was happy to see him, but there was not a trace of a smile on his master's face. Mr. Watkins turned away from Larry as he turned to face the truth. The two times tomorrow goodness was only a fiction. It was never going to turn into a reality. He walked toward the city park with his head down as Larry barked at a slow-moving pigeon on the sidewalk.

Mr. Watkins sat down at one of the picnic tables and felt the coldness of the seat on his thin legs. He had no more plans in his weary head. He felt the cold steel in his right pocket as he stared up at the sky, then spoke. "Larry, maybe I was wrong about this going to be a two times tomorrow good day. Maybe I was wrong when I thought that God had wanted me to keep giving my Social Security check to that hospital for burned children. Maybe I ain't in my right mind anymore."

Larry sat very still looking up into the face of the man he loved with all his heart, and for a moment it was as though Larry really could understand the words that fell from the mouth of his master. Larry whined as Mr. Watkins pulled the pistol from his pocket.

"Now, Larry, I want you to understand that this isn't your fault," Mr. Watkins said as he placed the pistol against his gray-haired temple. "I think maybe someone will take you home with them and feed you, Larry, so don't you worry. Ain't no need in both of us going hungry. You just wait and see, Larry, it'll be a two times tomorrow day before the sun sets. Now, you turn your head, Larry. I don't want you to see this." Mr. Watkins pulled the hammer back on the small pistol, but Larry would not look away. Larry sat there looking directly into Mr. Watkins's eyes.

Mr. Watkins began to cry. "I told you not to look at me, Larry. I can't do this if you keep looking at me. Now, stop it, please!"

Larry sensed something was awfully wrong with his master and began to bark loudly as his eyes stared intently at Mr. Watkins. A woman heard the commotion and began walking toward them as Mr. Watkins uncocked the hammer and quickly slid the pistol back into his overcoat pocket.

"Is this dog scaring you?" the woman asked with a concerned look on her face.

"Oh, no, ma'am," he hurriedly answered, "that's my own dog. His name is Larry."

"Well, if you say so," she replied, "but he sure seemed upset to me." She turned to leave, then suddenly whirled back around. "You look familiar to me," she said with a smile. "What's your name?"

"My name's Watkins," he said, "Herbert Watkins."

"Haven't I seen you over at the Children's Burn Center?" she inquired as she looked closely at him.

"Maybe so," he said. "I'm over there sometimes, but I don't stay long because they won't let me bring Larry inside, so I have to hurry back out to him." She leaned over and petted the dog.

"My name is Harris, Margaret Harris. I'm the chairperson of the fund-raising committee at the hospital," she said as she continued to pet Larry. Suddenly she turned her head to one side. "I know that name, Herbert Watkins. You're the man who has been giving us his Social Security check for the last several months. You're a most generous man!" she exclaimed.

Mr. Watkins didn't know why, maybe it was her gentle manner that evoked the truth, but he began to tell Mrs. Harris that he and Larry were hungry and they sure would like something to eat. He also told her that he was most sure that God had wanted him to donate his Social Security checks to help the children who had been badly burned and disfigured. He even took a deep breath and told her what a foolish thing he would have done if he could have gotten Larry to look the other way. He told her it was most fortunate that she had come along when she did.

Mrs. Harris stood there in reverent silence. Tears began to softly roll from her eyes as she gazed upon the old man and his faithful dog.

"Mr. Watkins, I am so happy to have met you this day. The truth is that I seldom come to this park by myself. Since my husband died I have busied myself in charity work so I don't have to think about my loneliness." Mrs. Harris once again leaned over to pet Larry. "I can see now I need to get out more often so I can meet nice people like you. My husband left me with a lot of memories and more money than I can ever spend, but I suppose I need to get on with life."

Mr. Watkins confirmed her comments with a nod. "Me, too," he said with a smile.

It was cold that night in Birmingham. Mr. Watkins's apartment was as empty as that old dog food can had been the night before. The servants' quarters behind Mrs. Harris's mansion had two new guests that night whose stomachs were full of steak and whose bodies were warm. It seemed most appropriate for two of God's servants to be housed there. As Mr. Watkins turned out the light, he placed his arm across Larry and gently spoke. "See, Larry, just like I told you. It's a two times tomorrow day."

You Can Have It

Accidents are often the acts of God
camouflaged in the cloak of chance.
UNKNOWN

Tim Myers was a kindhearted young man who grew
up with a giving attitude. He shared his toys with his
playmates, and if he had candy, he was quick to offer
that, also. He didn't have a selfish bone in his body. After
he graduated from high school, he got a manual labor job
to help pay his way through college. If Tim had any
money left over after his college expenses, he would give
the extra to his mama, who had raised him since his
father had died in Vietnam. Tim was forever helping
people with their college assignments and becoming a

brilliant student who offered to share his knowledge with anyone seeking it. He was a rare individual for sure, and his future was full of bright promises of bigger and better things to come. Then came that Thursday morning when Tim Myers lost touch with reality as he suffered a mental breakdown that nobody could have foreseen coming.

Tim was taken to the emergency room by his mama, who seemed as frightened as he did, as she wrung her hands and waited for the doctor to call her in and tell her what was wrong with her son. The doctor's face was solemn as he told Mrs. Myers that her son had suffered a psychotic break from reality, possibly schizophrenia, and would have to go to the state mental institution for further treatment. She looked over at Tim, who was lying on an exam table with a faraway look in his eyes. The Haldol was beginning to take effect as it curled him up into the chemical straitjacket that kept him calm. Mrs. Myers watched her Timmy as the drugs turned him into a zombie before she placed him in the front seat of her car and transported him to the state hospital.

Tim Myers's mind was broken, and horrible visions came there to viciously haunt him. He saw frightening things that were not there and heard accusing voices that no one else could hear. These hallucinations caused fear to pulse through his body as he knew, any moment, something dreadful was going to happen to him. He was a pitiful sight as he paced up and down the hall with wide eyes and narrow steps, the result of his fear and the major tranquilizers that were fighting to slow down his movements and his mind. Days passed, but Tim didn't seem to remember what they were or where he was, for that matter.

His mother came to visit, but she left each time wondering when her Timmy would appear behind the expressionless mask of a face she had never seen before. Weeks turned into months, and there was minimal improvement in his behavior as time went past. Finally, the doctors said she could take him home as long as he stayed on his medication and went to see a psychiatrist once a week. Mrs. Myers had taken a son into the emergency room but was taking home a stranger from the state mental hospital.

If love could have made Tim better, he would have been well in less than a week. Mrs. Myers showered him with kindness and attention, but Tim's mind always seemed to be somewhere too far away for her to reach. He no longer spoke about college and began to hoard all of his belongings in the closet in his room. He hid food under his bed and then forgot about it, until Mrs. Myers complained of the smell coming from his room. He'd go get it and sit in a stupor on the edge of the bed and try to eat the food, which she had to forcefully take from his hands. The rancid odor didn't seem to bother Tim, who wasn't sure why he had not been allowed to eat the rotten food.

At night, Mrs. Myers heard Tim talking out loud to people that she knew did not exist, except in his twisted mind. Mrs. Myers talked out loud at night also, but her words were spoken in prayers that she trusted would someday find the ears and heart of God.

Each week, Tim's mama would take him to see the psychiatrist, who would dispense prescriptions and advice. Mrs. Myers believed the psychiatrist was not that interested in her son's case, and she wasn't too sure the psychiatrist wasn't a little bit crazy himself. She noticed that every time his pipe went out, he became frustrated and would totally disregard her until it was safely lit again, which would bring a silly smile to his face as though he had accomplished something significant. After leaving the doctor's office, she would tell Tim that if he was normal, he would have been made crazy by now from seeing that wacky psychiatrist. Tim would almost smile a wax museum smile as his mama drove him home.

Spring came, but Tim did not notice the beauty. By now he hardly ventured from his room. His fears fought the drugs, and some nights they won as he lay in bed and waited for that unknown demon to come in the window and take what remained of his mind. Tim always thought it somewhat of a miracle when he awoke in the mornings and could still remember who he was and where he lived. Often, when the nights were the longest, his mama would come into his bedroom and rock him in her arms as though he were still a little boy with little boy fears.

Summer came, but Tim Myers's illness would not go away no matter how much medication he took.

Fall had arrived early that year and the smells of autumn were in the air. Burning leaves and the smoke from fireplaces were old familiar odors to Tim as he inhaled their unique fragrance through his bedroom window. He opened the window enough to let the smells in but not high enough to let in those awful demons that lurked no further from him than his mind. The leaves changed into beautiful colors, while it seemed nothing on this earth could change Tim back into the way he once was.

Mrs. Myers had never been much of a churchgoer, and, even if she had, she couldn't have risked leaving Tim alone at home by himself. Out of desperation one day, she looked up the number of a local church and dialed the pastor's office. To her surprise, the minister answered the telephone. Before long she was telling him all about her son and his problem. The minister asked her if it would be acceptable to place her and her son on a prayer list so that his church could pray for her son. Reluctantly, she told him that she had tried praying but with no results so far. The minister said it couldn't hurt anything to try, and she agreed and said she would be most appreciative, then, if he would place her son on that list.

Shortly after this, Tim became sicker than ever and Mrs. Myers was afraid she would have to take him back to the state hospital. On top of this, Tim came down with a bout of the flu. Fearing pneumonia, she took him to the family doctor, who immediately placed him in the local hospital for x-rays and treatment.

As sometimes happens, the radiology department was busy. By mistake Tim, who was to receive lung x-rays, instead received an MRI on his head and brain. The head studies were intended for a Tom Meyer. The mistake was caught and the correct x-rays were taken, but an alert radiologist decided to view Tim's MRI results as a teaching tool for a doctor serving his radiology residency at the hospital. It was then that the brain tumor was discovered.

Several days later, a neurosurgeon removed the plum-sized tumor from the troubled brain of Tim Myers and the biopsy indicated it was not malignant. Mrs. Myers was glad that Tim had been on that prayer list. Three days later she was sitting in the hospital room with her son when his lunch was brought in to him.

"That roast beef looks good enough to eat," Mrs. Myers said with a smile, trying to cheer up Tim, who looked at her with peaceful eyes.

"You can have it, Mama," he said with a big smile on his face. "I know you must be hungry from waiting so long for me to wake up."

It was the first time in what had seemed like forever that Tim had sounded like himself.

"How do you feel, Tim?" she asked with surprise in her voice.

"Mama, I feel absolutely great," he said. "In fact, I feel like taking a long walk in that beautiful weather out there." He nodded toward the window.

"But aren't you afraid of going outside, honey?" Mrs. Myers hesitantly inquired in her gentle manner.

"Oh, Mama, why in the world would I be afraid to go outside?" he asked with a laugh.

Mrs. Myers began to laugh herself as she realized that her son, Timmy, had come back to her. "Oh, I'm just cutting up with you," she replied as she touched his hand and he squeezed back just like the lovable son she had always known.

Mrs. Myers left the hospital that night with the doctor's explanation that evidently it was the tumor that had caused Tim to become so mentally disturbed. The doctor went on to say it was an administrative accident that had allowed them to discover the tumor in the first place. Mrs. Myers nodded her head in agreement with the doctor, but in her heart she knew that what had occurred was by no means an accident.

Cooking Up Some Conscience

"Even when there is no law, there is conscience."
Publilius Syrus

❧

It was a Wednesday in February of 1960, the best I can recollect. I was living with Grandma Allen, who lived by the Good Book. The cold weather was making it impossible to go to the park and shoot basketball on the outside court, so, after school, I would come home and study and busy myself until suppertime. One day, I had finished studying and wandered into the kitchen to see what she was preparing for supper. There were two pots on the stove and corn bread in the oven while an empty skillet sat on the front eye with nothing in it.

"What's for supper, Grandma?" I asked her as she put some salt in one of the pots.

"Black-eyed peas, boiled potatoes, and corn bread," she answered, putting the lid back on the pot.

"What you gonna cook in the skillet?" I asked her, hoping it might be fried pork chops.

Grandma turned and gave me her undivided attention before she spoke. "I'm cooking up some conscience," she said with a smile. I stood there with my mouth open having absolutely no idea what she was talking about. She saw my confusion and her smile just got bigger.

"What's wrong with you, Johnny, the cat got your tongue?" she asked me.

"No, ma'am," I sort of stuttered, "I guess I just don't understand what you mean, Grandma." Grandma Allen instructed me to sit down while she walked over to the refrigerator and got down a box from the top of the refrigerator. She pulled out what I thought was a plant that Aunt Margaret had brought back from her trip to Florida. I imagined that Grandma was saving it for sentimental reasons.

"What kind of plant is that, Grandma?" I asked her.

"This," she proudly spoke, "is a palm branch and these here leaves are what I'm fixing to cook," she informed me with a sense of reverence in her voice.

"Grandma, I don't mean to be rude," I quickly said, "but just fix some of that for yourself if you don't mind. I don't care to be eating no leaves!" When I said this, Grandma laughed so hard she started coughing. Finally, she regained her usual composure.

"Oh, Johnny, we ain't going to eat these leaves for supper. This is Ash Wednesday and I'm going to cook these leaves in that there skillet until some ashes form, and then I'm going to rub some on my forehead to remind me of the beginning of that time for soul-searching before Easter," Grandma Allen said to me.

I was pretty ignorant about such matters and thought perhaps the ashes were some kind of Indian ritual that Grandma Allen was fixing to perform. "Grandma Allen, I have no idea what you're talking about," I sincerely said. Grandma came and sat down with me at the kitchen table and began to strip the crumbling leaves from the branch.

"I'm sorry, Johnny," she apologized, "I shouldn't have laughed so hard. Maybe it would help you if I tried to explain it to you."

"I sure would appreciate that, Grandma Allen," I said, since my curiosity had been aroused by now.

"Today is a special day, Johnny," she began. "Today is Ash Wednesday, the first day of Lent, which lasts forty days before Easter. It is a time of spiritual preparation for Easter in remembrance of the passion, death, and resurrection of Jesus Christ. These here palm leaves are to remind us of Palm Sunday, the week before Easter, when Jesus entered the city of Jerusalem and the people spread palm leaves before Christ as he came riding into the city on a donkey. Do you understand so far?" she asked me.

"I understand about the leaves reminding us about Him coming into Jerusalem, but I don't understand why you burn them to ashes and then smudge them on your forehead," I honestly said to Grandma Allen. "What's that all about?" I asked her.

"Well, that smudge of ashes on our heads is to remind us of that old verse that we came from dust and will return to dust," she solemnly said. "It reminds us that we are humans and someday our lives will be over. It also reminds us that we are full of sin and sorrow and failure. I guess you might say it reminds us not to get too big for our britches and maybe it's best we be thinking about the Lord instead of those selfish concerns we get all wound up in that make us forget the Lord."

"So what is this Lent stuff, Grandma Allen?" I questioned. "What's it all about?"

"Well, that's when we fast or pray extra hard or give up something to show our respect for what God has done for us. We do it for forty days and I guess that is because Jesus fasted for forty days when He was in the wilderness. Did I help you on any of this?" Grandma wanted to know.

"Well, Grandma, I ain't sure. You know, it's a lot like

shooting basketball. You can talk about it all day long to somebody who ain't ever played before, but until they've actually shot a basketball, they won't know what it is like," I told her, hoping I wouldn't hurt her feelings.

"That's a good explanation, Johnny," she praised me. "I couldn't have put it better myself."

"Thank you, Grandma Allen," I said as I started to get up from the table. She motioned for me to stay seated as she waved downward with her hand.

"What is it, Grandma?" I asked her as I sat back down.

"Do you want to observe Lent with me this year, Johnny?" she seriously asked.

I didn't know what to say to Grandma Allen, but I supposed it would please her, so I told her, "Sure."

"That's wonderful," she said, as she stood up from the table, walked over to the stove, turned on the eye, and placed the leaves in the skillet. Suddenly, she turned and stared at me. "Johnny, I want you to know that usually the priest or minister administers the ashes, but when I was a child on the reservation, we were not allowed to attend the downtown churches, so the leader of the tribe performed the service. My church doesn't perform this service, so I do it myself. I'm telling you this because I don't want you to think that I'm being uppity."

"Oh, Grandma Allen, I would never think that," I assured her.

The palm leaves didn't smell so good, but when

Grandma Allen smudged the ashes on my head, I felt clean and good. She said those "dust to dust" words, and, to tell you the truth, I guess that was the first time I realized that someday I would die and that I hadn't lived up to what God probably had expected from me. I became most aware of Christ's sacrifice that day and felt ashamed of my own selfishness. I suppose you might say my conscience was bothering me, but I reckon that was part of the ritual right along with the feeling good part.

That was the Wednesday that Grandma and I decided to give up meat for forty days to honor Jesus. It sure was hard giving up hamburgers, but the hardest thing would have been to disappoint God or Grandma Allen. So, I gave up my hamburgers and meat of all kinds, and Grandma and I prayed every night. When I was alone in my bedroom, I told God those things I was too ashamed for Grandma Allen to hear or even know about.

That was a fine time in my life and I believe that was the purest I have ever felt in my heart in my entire life. When I left Grandma Allen's house later on that spring, it was like I had total amnesia and completely forgot all about Ash Wednesday, and Lent, and palm leaves, and Easter, and God, too, I suppose. Out on my own, I began to sow all my wild oats and somehow thought I was too sophisticated to continue the old-time religion that Grandma Allen had so painstakingly taught me. What a fool I was, running around trying to find heaven on earth. I now realize when your conscience isn't hurting you, especially when it should be, that you are in for a whole lot of pain.

Grandma Allen was right, just like she always was. That day with the palm leaves she was "cooking up some conscience" just like she had said she was. I spent many a year being a starving sinner, but these days my hunger is being fed by the memory of her spiritual words and my sincere desire to make sure I never again forget the recipe for happiness.

Easter Lessons in East Birmingham

*"One thing you can keep
and not be selfish is your word."*
ANONYMOUS

E ast Birmingham was an industrial neighborhood and home to the numerous black and white families who lived there and scratched out a living in the factories and foundries and mills.

These were places where hard work and hard men met each other head-on, and the companies signaled their presence in the community with giant smokestacks that sent up billowing clouds of black and gray smoke, which darkened the sky on windless days. Grandma and Granddaddy Allen lived in East Birmingham, but Granddaddy didn't work in any of the plants. Instead, he was a carpenter who often worked outside the neighborhood on houses and other buildings that were under construction. Granddaddy used to say, referring to the foundries, "Those places look too much like hell to suit my taste," and he wanted to be outdoors and away from the fiery furnaces and production lines that made products and broke men.

I spent many a summer in East Birmingham with Grandma and Granddaddy Allen, where they forged me like a piece of steel in one of those factories and Grandma put me on her anvil, trying her best to hammer me into the shape of something resembling a decent human being. After Granddaddy's death, the burden fell on Grandma's shoulders to complete the task they had both begun. She may have been old, but she still could swing a mighty mean hammer.

It was the Easter season of 1960. Grandma and I were sitting out on the front porch talking. It was during that spring when she had performed the Ash Wednesday ritual and we had given up meat for Lent, and I had a lot more hormones than sense in my seventeen-year-old body. I was trying to welsh on my promise of not eating meat and was hoping I could get Grandma Allen to release me from my obligation to keep my word.

"I'd sure like to have a big cheeseburger, Grandma," I said in a pitiful voice. "I can taste it right now," I continued talking, "with all that melted cheese and lettuce and tomato. I can even smell it, Grandma," I concluded, as I powerfully inhaled the evening air.

Grandma Allen pursed her lips, a sign of irritation I had learned, before she plainly spoke. "Get thee behind me, Satan," she said, informing me I had been trying to tempt her.

"Oh, Grandma, I was only teasing," I said, trying to weasel out of my words now that I had seen that they had upset her and she was displeased with me.

"Johnny, what am I going to do with you?" she asked, shaking her head from side to side in obvious frustration with me. "First you try to back out on your word to God, and then you try tempting me by talking about that cheeseburger, and now here you are lying to me about being only teasing when I know you weren't." Grandma Allen stared at me. My goodness, her stare could humble Hitler. I had to look away from her. I felt my face flush with embarrassment. I truly was at a loss for words, but Grandma Allen sure wasn't as she continued.

"Johnny, there's hamburger meat in the freezer, and if you want one, then go on in the kitchen and cook you one!" Her voice pierced the evening air and sounded as loud as one of those air raid signals we used to have in school when we would get beneath our desks. I was thinking how nice it would be to have a desk to hide beneath so Grandma Allen couldn't see me right then. I didn't answer her as I sat there wondering how Grandma Allen could always see through me as though I were made of glass. She would have made a great baseball umpire because she always called it just like she saw it. The truth was, I had been off base and Grandma had called me out and there was nothing subtle about her decision. I sat there in shame.

"Well, Johnny, make up your mind, what are you going to do?" Grandma demanded to know.

"I've changed my mind, Grandma Allen, I don't want a cheeseburger," I truthfully said in a low voice, "and I apologize for being a welsher and a tempter and a liar." As soon as I said those words, I couldn't believe I had done all those things in the amount of time it takes for a lightning bug to flash in the evening sky. My face gave me away.

"What's wrong with you, Johnny?" Grandma asked. "Are you all right?" she inquired.

"I guess so," I answered, "I just never knew that I could sin so fast." When I said this, it brought a knowing smile to Grandma Allen's face, then a sweet chuckle.

"It don't take long," Grandma confirmed my words, "but you're just a tadpole, Johnny, so I reckon you'll slow down as you get older. Besides, I love you and always will no matter what you do, so you just stop that fretting, you hear me," she concluded.

I nodded a "yes" to her.

Grandma Allen rocked in her high-back rocker for the longest time before she spoke again. "You know, Johnny, when you get out on your own you'll not be having anybody to tell you what to do. You'll be the boss of your own life and you'll be the one making the decisions. I know that sounds good to you, but sometimes it just ain't easy."

"I can see that, Grandma," I replied, "but I sure hope I do better than I did tonight."

"You will, Johnny," she reassured me, "but you might as well know that each person has to go through their own Easter experience." Grandma Allen then fell silent, waiting for me to ask her what she meant.

"What do you mean, Grandma Allen, about each person having to go through their own Easter experience?" I asked her for a clarification.

Grandma Allen smiled, perhaps figuring I was at least teachable. "The way I see it, Johnny," Grandma began, "is that we all go through a period in our lives when we have our trials, just like Jesus did. Most of the time, however, it ain't because we been doing good but rather doing bad. That's the time we look at ourselves and see we have been sinning and we look at ourselves mighty close and bring out all those facts, especially the ones that only we know, to prove to ourselves that we need to change. We sort of put our own selves on trial, do you understand?" she asked.

"I think I do, Grandma Allen," I answered, "but I'm afraid I would find myself guilty if I did that."

Grandma Allen smiled. "We all do," she stated, "and then we have to undergo our own suffering and crucify those parts of us that keep us from living the way that God intended for us to do. Sometimes it hurts as though we were driving nails into our own souls."

"What happens next, Grandma Allen?" I asked her, remembering the cheeseburger.

"Well, I figure we've got to bury our old self because, in a way, it's dead anyway since it's been put on trial and convicted and crucified," Grandma explained. "My grandfather, Two Skies, when he stopped drinking alcohol, buried a new bottle of whiskey at the tribal cemetery as a reminder of the death of that part of himself that needed to die."

"Now that's different, Grandma!" I exclaimed, and she smiled. "So, what is the next thing, the resurrection?" I asked her.

"Exactly, Johnny," she complimented me on my understanding. "Just like it says in the Good Book over there in Second Corinthians, 'therefore if any man be in Christ, he is a new creature: old things are passed away; behold, all things are become new.' So, now you have it, Johnny, every person sort of goes through his or her own personal Easter. So, what do you think?"

"I think I'm going into the kitchen and cook me up a big cheeseburger," I announced to Grandma Allen as she sat there too stunned to speak.

It took a while, but finally I returned to the front porch with the cheeseburger on a paper plate in one hand and a large kitchen knife in the other. Grandma Allen had the saddest look on her face as though her words had meant absolutely nothing to me.

"Would you like half, Grandma Allen?" I politely asked, teasing her by placing the knife at the center of the sandwich and smiling at her. Before she could answer, I quickly added, "I hope not 'cause I'm fixing to bury it!" I went down into the front yard and dug a hole with the butcher knife and buried the cheeseburger. I know smiles are silent, but I swore I heard Grandma Allen smiling as she rocked on the porch that evening.

Grandma Allen didn't live long enough to see me turn into a prodigal son, and I'm grateful for that; but her words lived long enough for me to realize that she was right about each of us having to go through his own trial, crucifixion, burial, and resurrection. It took a long time, but I guess I'm not alone in this process, sometimes taking many years. These days, I wouldn't mind or be ashamed if Grandma Allen was right there with me, watching me as I go through the day. In fact, some days I feel sure that she is.

Walking with Wisdom

The price of wisdom is beyond rubies.
JOB 28:18 NIV

———

The other night I was browsing through my bookshelves trying to find a book I had been looking for so I could get the correct quote I needed for a talk I was preparing to give. Unable to find it, I thought perhaps someone had borrowed it and it had not been returned. I sure wanted to find it since it contained a quote defining love as being any behavior that increases the spiritual growth of another human being. It was a book written by Dr.

Scott Peck, and I decided to scan the shelves one more time to ensure myself I hadn't overlooked it in my initial search. I was kneeling down examining the last bottom shelf when I came upon an aged black Bible which had a zipper that tightly closed around the cover of the book. It was a fine-looking Bible for sure, and I pulled it from the shelf and unzipped the dark-grained cowhide cover. Opening the Bible to the front pages, I read the faded inscription written in pencil. "To my beloved grandson, Johnny, Merry Christmas 1959, from Grandma Allen." I leafed through the pages and a smile came to my face when I thought that Grandma Allen would have been most pleased to see me down on my knees with a Bible in my hand. Standing up, I carried the old Bible over to my chair and sat down as my mind turned the pages of my memory back to those days of my youth when I was living with Grandma Allen in her white-framed house in east Birmingham.

Grandma Allen was a living example of Dr. Peck's definition about love being any behavior that increases the spiritual growth of another human being. She was always encouraging me to read the Bible and to do the right thing by people. Her concept of life was most simple. Love God and love your neighbor and everything else will work itself out. Grandma Allen wasn't much for this newfangled thing called situational ethics in which the rightness of a person's behavior is determined by the situation. To her, there never was any gray area. Right was right and wrong was wrong and there would be no excuses accepted. I remember the winter before she gave me this Bible. I was playing basketball, and she would walk the thirteen blocks to the high school to watch me play. Then she and I would walk home together after the game. I sure loved those times.

One night in December of 1959, I was preparing to leave early so I could get to the high school on time for the pregame meeting and Grandma was getting ready to eat supper before she left to come watch me play. She had just sat down at the table and had bowed her head to say grace when I interrupted her to tell her something I thought was important.

"Grandma Allen, I know that God listens to you, so I want you to ask Him something for me when you bless the meal," I said as I stuffed my uniform down into my carry bag.

I could tell she was a little perturbed that I had interrupted her prayer, but she calmly raised her head and looked me squarely in the eyes before she asked, "What exactly would it be that you want me to ask of God, Johnny?"

"Well, Grandma," I said, "I would like for you to ask Him to let us win the game tonight. It is for the city championship and a mighty important game. After all," I went on, "He really does seem to answer your prayers."

I stood by the table and watched as Grandma Allen's countenance changed and she fought to maintain her composure.

"I'll do nothing of the sort!" she declared, as she narrowed her eyes and stared at me in disbelief. "Don't you think God has more important things to do than bother with the outcome of some game? If you want me to thank God that you had food to eat tonight or a place to lay your head, then I'll do that. If you want me to praise Him that you have healthy legs to run and jump, then I'll do that, too. If you want me to ask Him to keep you safe from harm, then I'll do that also, but I sure ain't going to ask the great God Almighty to let your team win a mere game. Are we clear about this, Johnny?"

"Yes, ma'am," I meekly offered. I was turning to leave when Grandma pushed her chair back from the table, stood up, and grabbed me in her arms.

"I love you, Johnny," she sincerely said, "and I don't want to hurt your feelings, but I want you to understand that I am serious about what I ask God to do for me." She ruffled my hair and then said, "Run on now. I have faith that you'll do just fine tonight. Look for me on the top row of the seats."

"I will, Grandma," I assured her, and I kissed her cheek before I left for the high school.

Grandma Allen sat on the top row of the bleacher seats in the gymnasium that night and she looked so proud. She really didn't love basketball, she didn't even understand the game, but she loved me and rooted as loud as anyone in there. As it turned out, we won the game rather easily and I wondered why in the world I had ever worried about the final outcome. I showered and put on my jacket and went to meet Grandma Allen, who was waiting inside the gym by the large double doors. She yelled when she saw me coming and called me "the champion," which brought a silly, embarrassed smile to my face. I was going to explain that basketball was a team sport, but I realized it would have made no difference to her. We pushed the doors open, entering the cold night, and began our walk home.

Even though Grandma Allen was tall and stately and a nimble, full-blooded Cherokee Indian, I didn't trust the dark, uneven sidewalks, so I held her arm as we walked home to guard against her possibly falling. As we passed beneath a streetlight on the avenue, I glanced over at her and she grinned back at me and squeezed my arm. It was the first time I had been acutely aware of the wrinkles on her face and that she was aging. She had a scarf tied around her head to protect her against the wind and cold, and it framed her dignified face in a most beautiful way. I held her arm tightly as we stepped down from the curb and crossed the street. I found myself lifting up on her arm as we came to the curb across the street. They say that love can blind a person, and maybe that's true, because that was the first time I can ever remember seeing Grandma Allen as an old lady. She sure wasn't frail, but I was glad to be holding on to her as we traveled home.

"It sure is a beautiful night, isn't it, Johnny?" she stated more than asked.

"It sure is, Grandma!" I brightly answered. "There must be a million stars in the sky tonight."

She paused for a moment, then said, "Well, that's a fact, but I wasn't thinking about the stars. I mean it's beautiful because you're so happy and I'm happy seeing you that way. But above all," she continued, "I'm proud of you for being such a good boy."

"Ah, Grandma, you're just prejudiced," I laughed. "You mean you are still proud of me after I hauled off and asked you to pray that our team would win the game tonight?" I teased.

I was afraid that Grandma Allen wasn't aware that I was only teasing because a most serious expression could be seen on her face as we passed beneath another streetlight. Suddenly, she pulled down on my arm for us to stop. We stood beneath the streetlamp as she caught her breath. In my excitement about the game, I suppose I had been walking too fast. In a few moments she had caught her breath and cleared her throat.

"Someday, Johnny, there will come a time when you can no longer run and jump. Your face will become wrinkled and the sounds of cheering crowds will only be a distant memory. Your body will be full of pain and your soul will ache over the hurts you have brought to yourself and others. You'll just wake up one day and realize you have lived most of your days and not that many remain anymore. When that time comes, you'll understand that praying to God is a most serious business and you won't care to be bothering Him with stuff that He doesn't think is very important. Don't you see, Johnny, we're only passing through this old world, and when it's all over, the only thing that is important is getting right with the great God Almighty. Do you understand?"

"Sure, Grandma," I said. "Are you ready to walk on home?"

"Okay," she said, "but go a little slower. The house will still be sitting there when we get home."

Grandma Allen was right. The house was still there when we came down the street. She was also right about getting older, although I had no idea what she was talking about that long-ago night as we walked home.

Nowadays, my body pains and my soul aches for all the ways I have hurt myself and others over the years. As I was kneeling down to put the Bible back on the shelf, I caught myself beginning to pray to God, thanking Him for letting me get right with Him once again, as well as for all the blessings He has brought my way. I know Grandma Allen would be proud of me for not praying for something as insignificant as a Tennessee victory in the Fiesta Bowl.

God's Big Acre

"Do not store up for yourselves treasures on earth,
where moth and rust destroy,
and where thieves break in and steal."
MATTHEW 6:19 NIV

W oodrow Wilson was his name, but there was no mistaking him for the former president, or any of his kinfolk, for that matter. He wore bib overalls and farmed a small patch of land outside of the city, which seemed to be growing toward him every day with fast-food restaurants and service stations springing up faster than kudzu on a summer day. His brothers had all gone to college, but not Woodrow, who preferred doing odd jobs and farming his little patch of land that had been left to him by his late father. The land sat right off the main highway and was a lucrative piece of business property that, if ever sold, would bring Woodrow a mighty pretty penny.

Before long, the whole area was going commercial and pressure was mounting from a shopping mall concern that kept raising its giving price since old Woodrow was not giving them an asking price. No matter how much they offered, he just shook his head and informed them he was not interested. The day they told him they were going to build a mall and had bought all the property around him and he was the only thing standing between them and a mall larger than many Alabama towns and they were prepared to give him $750,000, well, that was the day Woodrow sat down to talk.

When the meeting between the men in the three-piece suits and Woodrow in his bib overalls was over, there were still a few problems to be ironed out. Seems the men wanted to use his land as a parking area and this insulted Woodrow, who expected a Sears store at the very least to be sitting on top of his one acre. Then there was that matter of money. Woodrow said he liked the sound of *one and a half* million dollars better than $750,000, and the men just couldn't believe he wasn't drooling on himself at their first offer. They said that was too much. He said their offer was too small. They balked. He knew mules. They knew malls.

Woodrow was holding up progress, but he didn't worry

about that. Construction on the mall was held up by his stubborn attitude and his reluctance to part with his land until his price was met. His brothers, who had no ownership in the land, started coming by more than usual. They would sit and try to convince Woodrow that if he sold his land, they would invest his money for him. Woodrow chuckled and said that when he sold his acre, he'd have so much money that he wouldn't need to invest a dime. Strange thing about how money makes people do weird things, and his brothers thought long and hard about having him committed. Finally, they gave up on that idea when he said he'd sell his property for five dollars if they tried that on him and that would prove him crazy, but by then it would be too late for them to get his money.

Time went by and Woodrow kept on farming. Sure the money would have been nice to have, but then again Woodrow really had no need for it. All he had was paid for and he never had owned a credit card or paid for anything on time except his insurance. Finally, the serious men in suits said they would pay him exactly $1 million for his property and that was their final offer, so take it or leave it. Woodrow put his thumbs in the breast pockets of his bib overalls and stared straight through the men before he spoke.

"I know y'all mean well and are looking after my best interests, but I reckon y'all don't know y'all were disrespectful by thinking I was some kind of 'Ned in the first reader' hick who would cave in at the first sight of a pile of money. Thank you for dropping by, gentlemen," he concluded as he walked them to the front door of his shotgun house. "I ain't selling."

The next day Woodrow called Ruford Pike, an old-time evangelist he knew who stayed in his trailer most of his time, except on those rare occasions when some church felt sorry for him and asked him to come preach at a one-day revival.

"Ruford, how'd you like to have your own church?" Woodrow began, and silence came on the other end of the telephone. "Ruford, if you're still alive, I want you to answer me," Woodrow demanded.

"Don't nobody want me to pastor a church, Woodrow," Ruford answered. "What in the world are you talking about?"

"Well, hear me out now, Ruford. It turns out my property is mighty valuable to those folks wanting to build a huge mall out where I live. I already refused a flat million dollars for it 'cause I know those taxes would just eat me alive. But I have an idea that you might be interested in helping me with and it will be of benefit to us both. Are you interested in listening?" Woodrow wanted to know.

"Never hurts to listen, Woodrow. What do you have on your mind?" a curious Ruford asked.

"Well, the way I figure it is that we can turn my old shotgun house into a small church, which I thought you might like to become pastor of, of course. I'd sell you a third of my property for a dollar, and you could ordain me as your assistant pastor. Then we'd hold on to the property until they agree to pay us a million and a half for it, and then we could avoid taxes since we were a church and all. Look, Ruford, my place was assessed two years ago and it's only worth $75,000. Course, that was before these mall people came along. Maybe we could work it out where we'd sell them the property for $75,000 and claim everything else above that was simply a donation to the church for relocation and a new building. Maybe the mall folks could write it off on their own taxes. If it works the way I got it figured, you'll have half a million and you can build your own church. I'll clear a million, tax-free. Well, that's it, Ruford. What do you say?" Woodrow waited for an answer.

"Are you sure this is all legal? I don't want to break the law, you know," Ruford stated.

"All legal I tell you. Ready for your own church, Ruford?" Woodrow inquired.

"Count me in, Woodrow. I'm ready when you are," came the happy answer.

That was how the Narrow Gate Church came to be. It got its name from the narrow-looking shotgun house it came to inhabit and, of course, it did relate to the Scriptures.

Now that his house had become a church, Woodrow

went to live with Ruford in his old trailer. Every Sunday Pastor Pike and Pastor Wilson opened the door to the new church and waited for new members to enter. Before long, Pastor Pike's preaching started to touch the few people who were showing up for church and they began to bring others. Pretty soon, the house was no longer large enough to accommodate the crowd of new members.

By now, the land developers for the mall had raised their offer to one and a quarter million dollars, but Woodrow was holding out for that other quarter of a million. When the new congregation members said there were enough carpenters and brick masons among them to put an addition on to the church at almost no cost, Woodrow told them to go ahead and get to building. Woodrow was seeing dollar signs, but Pastor Pike was seeing a completely different set of signs that he supposed was from God, especially as the church family continued to grow at an unbelievable pace.

No sooner was the new addition completed, than the members had to start construction on another one because people were joining the church as though they were enlisting for a war. There was a war of sorts going on, especially in the minds of Woodrow Wilson and Ruford Pike.

"Well," Woodrow began, "I heard from the developers and they have finally agreed to our asking price of one and a half million. How about that, Ruford?" he asked. "Are you ready to be a rich man?"

Ruford pressed his lips together and rubbed them with his hand. "Woodrow, haven't you been noticing what's been going on right before our very eyes? We're in the middle of the most rapidly growing church I ever heard of. I don't think this is no accident. I think maybe God is telling us something, don't you?"

"Maybe so, Ruford. You know a whole lot more about the Lord than I do, but that sure is a lot of money to be turning down. Don't you want to be rich?" Woodrow asked him.

"Well, to tell you the truth, Woodrow, the other night I got to thinking about what Christ said about how hard it is for a rich man to enter the kingdom of God, and it frightens me to think I might be making money more important than the Lord. Whatever I'm saying in that pulpit is coming from God and that's why this church has grown. I truly believe that God wants us to keep doing His work right here! Woodrow, I sure wish you loved the Lord as much as you do that money you keep talking about." Ruford's voice was full of emotion.

His friend Woodrow placed his hands on Ruford's shoulders. "Oh, Ruford, you always was a better preacher than a businessman," Woodrow honestly said. "Goodness, it's only money. I reckon I'm too old to start worrying about somebody trying to beat me out of my newfound wealth, anyway. Besides, at my age, maybe it's best for me to be storing up treasures in heaven. You win, Ruford.

I'll call tomorrow and tell them we ain't selling at any price," Wood-row promised with purpose in his voice. Ruford sighed and smiled.

They never did build that shopping mall out near Woodrow's land. It was a good thing they didn't, because it turned out that the Narrow Gate Church needed room for expansion. The majority of land surrounding Wood-row's acre is now owned by the church and, counting the church's two top floors, the Narrow Gate Church has more square feet in it than that mall would have had if it had been built. God took that one little acre and made it big for a purpose.

"One thing is certain," Pastor Ruford Pike is fond of saying, "you can't find salvation at the mall." Maybe that's why salvation never goes out of style. At the Narrow Gate Church, Woodrow and Ruford may still be in sales, but they know for certain that God is still in management.

A Cup of Sugar for the Soul

"Love your neighbor as yourself."
MATTHEW 22:39 NIV

Mrs. Lopresti lived down the street from Grandma Allen when I was just a young boy. In the summers, I would come to Grandma's house to live. It's strange how, when we are children, each new person we meet leaves a vivid picture in our minds and eyes as though we were recently cured from blindness and each thing we see seems so fresh and wonderful. It was that way with my meeting Mrs. Lopresti.

Mrs. Lopresti was a young woman with three small children of her own. They were too young for me to play with, and I would usually see them and their mother when they came over to Grandma's house to borrow sugar or cornmeal or some kind of spice. Grandma Allen always seemed to be happy with their coming, and we would all sit on the front porch in the summertime and talk for the longest time. Grandma Allen would usually have her old Bible lying in one of the rockers and was quick to pick it up and share with Mrs. Lopresti what she had been reading. Mrs. Lopresti seemed curious as she listened to Grandma explain the words of God, something that Grandma did with great enthusiasm and intensity. Sometimes it was almost as though Grandma thought she was a preacher involved in a war for Mrs. Lopresti's soul, and she was not reluctant to use the Bible as a weapon. As I remember it, that old Bible was big enough and heavy enough to have qualified as one. That whole summer I watched as Grandma Allen gave Mrs. Lopresti sugar and cornmeal and vegetables from the garden and, of course, God's Word.

I never heard Grandma Allen say any bad words against Mrs. Lopresti, but that was not the case with her neighbors, especially Mrs. Myers. Mrs. Myers was a widow woman who lived three houses down from Mrs. Lopresti, and she would come to talk to Grandma Allen in the late afternoons when the sun was setting and it was cool enough for her to get out and walk. Mrs. Myers was older than Grandma, but her mouth seemed mighty young, as she would talk almost nonstop while she sat in one of the front porch rockers telling Grandma what was wrong with Mrs. Lopresti.

"You do know that her husband left her," Mrs. Myers said with raised eyebrows, "and he ain't coming back, either."

"I know," Grandma answered. "It must be terribly difficult raising children without a father."

"Well, she seems to be doing all right for herself, if you ask me," Mrs. Myers sternly said. "I saw her coming home the other night with some man and it sure wasn't her husband. I suppose she left her three little children with a strange baby-sitter while she went out on a date. I can't believe she has the gall to come borrow sugar and stuff from you if she has enough money to waste on a sitter so she can go out and kick up her heels."

"Well, I don't reckon it hurts for a young woman like her to have a little fun," Grandma said with a smile. "After all," Grandma continued, "she's in need of a new husband to help her raise and support her children. I don't see any harm in what she's doing."

"You're so naive, Mrs. Allen," Mrs. Myers bristled. "It's a different man every time from what I can tell. I think that Lopresti woman ain't nothing more than a hussy, I tell you. It's pure shameful the way she acts. I can't stand to see her acting like a streetwalker and then coming over here to take advantage of your kindness by borrowing food from you. She's treating you like a fool," Mrs. Myers concluded, with a finger pointed at Grandma Allen for emphasis.

Grandma Allen told me to take myself into the kitchen and fix myself a peanut butter and jelly sandwich to tide me over until supper. I told her I wasn't hungry; but when she gave me her "do as I say" look, I got up and opened the screen door and entered the house. Once I was inside the house, I hid against the wall next to the door so I could hear what was being said. I knew Grandma Allen would kill me if she knew what I was doing, but my curiosity was stronger than my fear, so I strained to listen to hear the words from the front porch.

"Mrs. Myers," I heard Grandma say with a firm voice, "I don't ever want you using those words you used around my grandson. He is too young to hear such stuff, and I won't ever allow it again. Are we clear on this?" I flattened myself against the inside wall. I knew that tone of voice was Grandma's "I mean business" tone and she wasn't in a good mood.

Mrs. Myers probably was in shock or fear because it took her a while before she answered.

"I apologize, Mrs. Allen," she said. "I guess I was so concerned about her taking advantage of you that I didn't choose my words carefully. I'm sorry if I offended you or your grandson."

Her words didn't seem to pacify Grandma Allen. "Mrs. Lopresti is my friend," Grandma simply stated, "and I've never heard her say a bad thing about anybody. The truth of the matter is that you are a nosy busybody who's got nothing better to do than find fault with somebody so you can feel superior. I'm an old woman with old ears and eyes, so don't try to pull the wool over my eyes, Mrs. Myers." Grandma's voice was very loud by now.

"Don't you take that tone with me," Mrs. Myers angrily replied. "It's not my fault that you think that you can take that old Bible of yours and turn a slut into a saint. You're an old fool, Mrs. Allen, and just hate to admit it."

Suddenly I could hear nothing but the sound of Grandma's rocker as she began to rock faster. I was just a kid, but even I knew that was the worst of all signs that Grandma Allen was at the end of her patience with someone.

"Mrs. Myers," Grandma Allen slowly and deliberately spoke, "there is nothing wrong with Mrs. Lopresti that time and the good Lord aren't going to take care of, and I have faith in that. However, it's you I worry about. I know your husband came home late many a night when he was still alive, and I have always chosen not to say anything to you about that secret in your life. It is time that you under-stand that this woman is not the same as your deceased husband, so you need to stop treating her as though she is trying to hurt you. I suggest you go on home and look in the mirror, and when you get a clear view of the beam in your eye, you may forgive the mote in Mrs. Lopresti's eye." I heard Grandma stand up from her rocker.

Mrs. Myers said not a single word as I heard her steps across the front porch then changing sounds as she went down the concrete steps. "You're still an old fool," Mrs. Myers said and added from a safe distance, "that girl ain't ever going to amount to nothing!"

The word "nothing" was still echoing in my head as I dashed toward the kitchen to quickly make a sandwich. I swore to myself that I would never let Grandma Allen know I had overheard the conversation with Mrs. Myers.

The summer flew past, just like all summers at Grandma Allen's white-framed house did. Mrs. Lopresti was a regular visitor, but Mrs. Myers never came back. Grandma Allen continued to share her "sugar for the soul" with Mrs. Lopresti right along with the cups of sugar and flour and cornmeal.

Mrs. Lopresti moved that fall, and I didn't see her again until the day of Grandma Allen's funeral many years later.

"Excuse me," the distinguished lady with gray hair said as I was walking toward my car after the burial service. "Are you Mrs. Allen's grandson, Johnny?"

"Yes, ma'am, I am," I solemnly answered, failing to recognize her. "I'm sorry, I don't remember your name," I apologized.

"I'm Gail Lopresti," she sweetly answered. "Your grandma was a friend to me many years ago. She was a most wonderful woman. She was always giving me a cup of sugar and a large helping of the Bible. I guess I remember her best for giving me hope and kindness."

"Oh, yes," I said, "I remember you now. You were really one of her favorite people. She always said God had something special in store for you."

"Well, she was right," Mrs. Lopresti said with a smile. "She had faith in me and it made me have faith in myself. I went back to college at her urgings and wound up marrying a young preacher over at Samford University. Sometimes I figure your grandma Allen may have been an angel sent to bring some light to my darkest days. I was pretty wild when I first met her, you know."

"I don't know anything about that," I lied with a smile, "but I suppose if you were, she knew how to tame you. That was an awfully big Bible she had." We both laughed as she left with a grin upon her face.

Some days, when life is so hard for me, I think of Grandma Allen and wish she were here to rock and read Scriptures to me. No matter how bitter life could become, it sure seemed that Grandma Allen always had a cup of sugar for the soul that she kept in that big old

Bible of hers and it could sweeten even the bitterest of times. Living with Grandma, my cup had forever run over, what with her pouring goodness into it each day. Come to think of it, how can my cup ever be empty as long as I have her memory to fill it up?

Giving What's Worth Keeping

"It is well to give when asked,
but it is better to give unasked,
through understanding."
KAHLIL GIBRAN

❧

Sometimes it seems so strange how the rule of the day is to be selfish. By selfish, I mean letting our lives revolve around ourselves as though we were the absolute center of the universe. As a result, certain attitudes are formed that reflect a subtle sickness in our society that has to do with the acquisition of material goods and a reluctance to share our good fortune with others less fortunate than us. In fact, there appears to be an attitude of anger towards those who are poor and who are seeking some relief from the poverty that pulls them down into the depths of depression. There is much discussion about "welfare mothers and their food stamps," and to live in a federal housing project is taken as proof that a person has failed at achieving the overvalued goal of economic success and financial independence. We sometimes look down our noses at folks who are shabbily dressed or drive old jalopies or live in substandard houses as though they are morally and constitutionally inferior to us. Yet, I can't seem to get the picture of Jesus using a Mercedes as His mode of transportation during His second coming. I reckon He won't be examining our bank accounts or the square footage of our houses or our stock portfolios or staring at our diplomas upon the wall. In fact, He might just be wondering why we would be prideful about such things if our neighbors were suffering and we had neglected to help them in their hour of need.

Being hungry or homeless or physically hurting and being powerless to change that situation must be a terrible place to be. "Show me the money" may be the catch phrase of the day, but I'm certain that will not be one of the questions that the Almighty will be asking us when it is all over. Instead, He probably will want to know what we have done to help the lost, the lonely, the least, and the lowest. Quite frankly, I'm afraid I would be looking down at the ground in shame as I tried to stammer out some lame excuse for being so selfish. After all, Grandma Allen taught me about giving many years ago, but I let her seeds of wisdom get choked out by not tending the garden of goodness that she worked so hard to plant in my fertile young mind. Sometimes it truly does feel like only yesterday that we were sitting on that old wooden front porch as I was preparing to leave her house to go off and play professional baseball. I had just graduated from high school, but Grandma Allen had had her Ph.D. in life for a mighty long time.

It was the month of May in 1960 and the warm breeze was a welcome relief after the cold winter. Grandma Allen was sitting in her favorite rocker reading her Bible, and I was reading the sports pages of the *Birmingham News*. I glanced up from the paper to see her engrossed in the Scriptures as her lips slowly moved while she read the words silently. Grandma Allen had a habit of moving her lips as she read, and I never saw that as a sign of her lack of education but rather as a signal to not interrupt her. When her lips stopped moving, I knew it would be all right for me to speak or ask her a question. Anyway, I found myself staring at her and realizing that her sweet face and demeanor made me feel as warm as the weather did. She was wearing a print house dress with pockets in it. Grandma liked dresses with pockets so she could carry her essentials such as tissue for her glasses and a tin of snuff and a pencil and paper so she could copy down those Bible verses she had questions about so the minister could explain them when he visited. I sat there admiring Grandma Allen and thinking about how much I would be missing her when I left to play baseball, but I also was thinking about the two new items she had begun to carry in her pockets on a regular basis. Granddaddy Allen had died many years before, but lately Grandma had taken his pocketknife and railroad watch from her hope chest and had been carrying them with her religiously, every day. She carried the pocketknife in her right pocket just like he had and his railroad watch in her left pocket with the top of the watch fob connected to the sash of her dress.

Grandma's lips were together as though she were keeping God's words from coming back out of her head, so I decided it was a good time to talk with her.

"Grandma Allen," I said as she shut her Bible to listen to me, "I sure am going to miss you when I leave."

"Well, you are coming back, aren't you?" she teased me.

"Of course I'm coming back," I answered, "but it won't be until the fall."

"In that case, since you're coming back, I guess I can rest easy," she declared as she pulled the watch up and out of her left pocket and gently opened the protective case and checked the time.

"What time is it, Grandma Allen?" I asked her as she sat staring at the watch of the man with whom she had lived her entire life.

"Well, this fine timepiece says it is 4:30," she replied as she snapped the cover closed. "Johnny, do you realize that your granddaddy must have held this watch thousands of times as he checked the time over the years. I like the idea of my hands holding something he valued so much. I imagine his very fingerprints are still on it," she concluded with a sigh and a smile.

"I betcha they are," I confirmed her words. "I remember all the times Granddaddy polished it with the silver polish to keep it bright and shiny. He sure loved that watch, didn't he, Grandma?"

"That he did," she wistfully answered. "I remember when he first became a carpenter and bought it so he would be sure that he got to the job on time, and he never quit work until he would check to insure it was the right time to come home. 'Time is all we really have,' he used to say and I suppose he was right." Grandma fell silent as she continued to stare down at the watch as though she were in deep thought.

"What are you thinking, Grandma Allen?" I softly questioned.

"I was thinking about how much I love this watch," she said, as she unhooked the fob from her sash and admired the watch hanging down from the chain. "And," she continued, "I was also thinking about how much I want you to have it."

At first, I didn't know exactly what to say. Finally some words came out. "Grandma Allen, I know how much you love that watch and I couldn't possibly take it."

Grandma Allen pursed her lips. My goodness, I hated it when she did that because it meant she was upset with me. "I couldn't take it, Grandma," I repeated, but she treated my words as though they didn't exist. She stood up from her rocker and told me to stand up.

"You will take this watch!" she declared as she attached the clasp of the chain to a belt loop on my blue jeans and gently slid the watch into my left pocket. "Your granddaddy loved you and would want you to have it. Now that settles it! I don't want to hear another word, you hear me?"

I thought of protesting but instead simply said, "Yes, ma'am."

Grandma returned to her rocker and picked up her Bible with a smile. Suddenly, my heart went out to her and I opened my mouth before she opened her Bible.

"Grandma Allen, I really wish you would be keeping this watch. I might lose it or break it and then I'd feel awful foolish about taking something I know you'd rather keep."

"Don't you go insulting me, Johnny!" she sternly said. "It's time you learned that giving something that you'd rather keep is the only true giving there is. How could I be giving you something valuable if I didn't want it as much as you do? If I gave you something I didn't want to keep, then it ain't much of a gift as far as I'm concerned. Do you understand?" she asked, as she opened her Bible.

"Yes, ma'am," I conceded, but I really was too young to truly grasp what she was telling me. I also was too ignorant of true generosity to understand why Granddaddy's pocketknife was in my suitcase when I arrived in Kingsport to play my first summer of professional baseball. There it was, snuggled down in the right front pocket of my good blue jeans.

Well, many years have been lived since that spring evening on Grandma Allen's front porch. I'm sad to report that, over the years, I lost the watch and the pocketknife. However, I imagine I am the saddest to report that I lost the meaning of what she had said about true giving. Grandma Allen was right. When we give what we really want to keep, then we are truly giving. Strange how giving until it hurts turns out to make a lot of sense, after all.

The Miracle on Boswell Road

God is our refuge and strength,
an ever-present help in trouble.
PSALM 46:1 NIV

It had all the makings of a tragedy. It was an event that all parents fear. A tenderhearted daughter caught up in a hardhearted depression that daily attempted to smother her soul. So, the search began for a daughter who had taken all of her potentially lethal medications, put them in an old brown lunch bag, and disappeared into the vast forest surrounding her parents' home in the country. Her mission, according to the suicide note found scribbled in her diary, was to take a huge overdose of the medicines she had taken with her into the woods. There was death in that brown bag. A hundred Xanax, a hundred Prozac, two hundred antiseizure capsules, and a can of diet cola to send them into her stomach.

It was the twenty-third of November 1996, the Saturday before Thanksgiving Day, when Ginger's depression prevented her from seeing the brilliant autumn forest. To her it was just one more black and white scene with no meaning. This day, there was nothing left for her to be grateful for except her anticipated escape from the accusing voices that tormented her without end. Some say suicide is a permanent solution to a temporary problem, but Ginger's problem had not been temporary. Two earlier suicide attempts had narrowly failed, but this time she was not going to be denied. Ironically, her parents had brought her home to take care of her after her second attempt. But the voices in her head had warned her not to tell her parents about them or they would invade her parents' minds and destroy them, also.

Ginger was only twenty-seven years old, but it was an ancient, tormented woman who had left to end her life. The voices had instructed her about what she was to do. "Tell your daddy you're going for a walk. He's watching the football game. Go get the medicines, put them in them in a brown sandwich bag, and hide them beneath your coat. Tell him you are feeling better and want to get some fresh air. Your mother is at the grocery store, so don't worry about her. Do as I tell you, Ginger!"

She did.

By evening, a rescue squad of about sixty men was in the woods searching. It already was dark and the night air was filled with the sound of bloodhounds barking. The dogs had picked up Ginger's scent from her pillowcase, and they were moving up to the left of the house as they sniffed and howled into the cold Tennessee night with men following them, thrashing through the thick woods. The roar of the searchers' numerous ATVs droned in the distance.

Inside the house was a dining room full of friends of Ginger's parents. They had come for the vigil and to offer support and prayers. Their attention turned to the rescue supervisor, who came into the room. He stood there catching his breath from his hurried approach to the house.

"We still haven't found her yet. We have the air- and ground-tracking bloodhounds leading the men. It's supposed to go down to freezing tonight. We're trying to find her before the drugs take complete effect, so we are doing all we can do. We have sectioned off the area and men are combing the woods all the way up to where the land borders the lake. Some more men and dogs are on the way." A message blared through his walkie-talkie. "I've got to go; I'll be back in a couple of hours if we haven't found her before then."

The friends joined hands and prayed as they sat around the old dining room table. It was a scene filled with reverence. They were not praying to sound good but rather to earnestly make contact with the great God Almighty. Ginger's parents were in shock—numbness had slackened their jaws and washed the color from their eyes. There were tears filled with hope that God would bring a triumph to that old farmhouse and that Ginger would be found alive. These were prayers that penetrated to the depths of each person present. Sometimes prayers can be as empty as the barren souls that utter them. But these prayers, well, they were the real McCoy. No pretense, no flowery words, no piety, no self-righteousness, nothing but words that sprang from the depths of their souls as they beseeched God for His divine intervention. Surely, God must have found pleasure in the voices that trusted their prayers to scale the walls to heaven. They knew God was listening to them at that very moment.

At midnight the rescue workers were exhausted. They had not found Ginger. The dogs had tracked to a spot where it seemed she had vanished into thin air. Was she abducted?

"Not likely," the rescue supervisor said. "We will be back here at sunrise to start again. We should have even more men tomorrow. I'm sorry. We have done all we can do tonight." As he left, the preacher arrived. He was late in getting the word about Ginger, but now he had come bringing God's Word. Prayers were lifted up to heaven in a powerful way as once again the family and friends sought God's guidance and comfort. Sincerity permeated the room. Earnest prayers were spoken by earnest people. It was a long time before the prayers were over, some folks praying twice as they went in a circle one after the other. Then the men stepped out on the back porch to talk.

Ginger's daddy was distraught and his face was drawn tight over his cheekbones. His brows furrowed as he spoke.

"We haven't lived here long enough to know which funeral home we should use. Who do you think. . . ?" he asked the men.

They gave their opinions. Despite their prayers, reality was falling upon them like the cold night dew. Ginger had been gone for eleven hours. It was supposed to go down to freezing. The woods were full of coyotes. The drugs should have overpowered her by now, as she lay somewhere unconscious and near death. Ginger's daddy, now fearing the worst, prayed that she was in God's arms where she would not be cold. He asked God to not let the coyotes eat her flesh—if she was with Him, then he knew she was finally at peace. Grown men cried. The Holy Spirit huddled the men together for more prayers. It was 2 A.M. before people found a place to sit or lay. It was three in the morning when Ginger's father screamed her name into the cold night air.

Sunday brought sunshine, blue skies, and over a hundred men and women to the farmhouse on Boswell Road. There were boats cruising the shoreline for any evidence of Ginger. A helicopter was flying overhead; its spotter was Tennessee Bureau of Investigation agent Larry Fowlkes-Davis. There were bloodhounds and German Shepherd cadaver dogs. God had sent a beautiful day for the search, which seemed to make the reality of what had happened seem even more tragic.

The church had been in constant prayer all morning for Ginger, but at noon on Sunday she still had not been found. The tired rescue crews broke for lunch. They had given up. They hadn't said the words, but their faces told the story. Finding her body was all they thought possible at this point.

Ginger's daddy stood in the front yard with his friend, Ron, who could hardly bear looking at the terror-filled faces of Ginger's parents.

After lunch, the rescue squad decided to search up to the right of the house. None of the dogs had tracked in that direction during the past twenty-four hours, but the rescue squad said it was worth a try.

Not more than fifteen minutes had passed when a commotion could be heard from up the road. Walkie-talkies crackled everywhere. It was obvious that something significant had happened. The rescue supervisor, with a serious expression on his face, began his approach toward Ginger's daddy. Her daddy's face was frozen in fear. A strange quietness filled the air and people stood still in their dreaded anticipation.

"Sir, we have found your daughter," the supervisor said, his face as still as the air. A lifetime passed as the man paused to listen to the inaudible report coming in on his handheld walkie-talkie.

His eyes cocked to his left as he placed it up to his ear. Ginger's daddy stood there with his arms down at his sides, his body and shoulders sagging toward the ground. Nothing left now but for the final pronouncement. Then the words came.

"Sir, she's alive!"

Her daddy's arms flew upward as his eyes riveted on the cloudless blue sky. He stretched on his toes as though he were attempting to touch the very hem of heaven. Those there will always vividly remember his howling. Several people thought she was dead as they heard his tremendous wailing rising up to the heavens like a frightened bird. His wife came running toward him with tears of joy being jostled from her eyes with every hurried step. They embraced and beyond their will fell to their knees upon the ground in exhaustion and gratitude as they yelled, "She's alive! She's alive!"

It was a beautiful sight to behold, especially when all their beleaguered friends rushed to join them, falling on their knees as they hugged everyone in celebration. It was quite a sight all right. Everywhere a person looked there were tears of joy. Strong-as-a-mule men with beards and dirty clothes were embracing and kissing each other. The preacher joined the crowd of people around Ginger's parents and began to pray.

"We know You don't work no half miracles, God. Be with Ginger as the ambulance takes her to the hospital and continue to work a miracle in her life. We praise Your name for what You have done and know You will bring her healing. Oh, in the precious name of Christ, we thank You. Amen."

The circle of people began to disperse for the trip to the hospital. None of them had seen Ginger yet; since she was so far into the woods the ambulance had to come in through a field on the far side to transport her. The ambulance siren began wailing in the distance. Surely, the attendants must have heard Ginger's daddy wailing before they sped off with her. A caravan of Christians drove the seventeen miles to the hospital.

Ginger was in good hands at the emergency room. She was going to live and the excitement and joy were evident among those gathered outside.

"The weatherman said it was going down to freezing last night, but it didn't; if it had, she would have frozen to death!" an older man said.

"She vomited up some of those pills," another said.

"They said her face was lying in it when they found her. If she had been on her back, she would have choked to death on her own vomit, I tell you!"

The man who had found Ginger spoke next with a quiet voice. "I found a dead coyote not more than fifty feet from where she lay. I examined that critter from head to toe and there wasn't a mark on it." He finished and shook his head from side to side in wonderment.

"Can you believe that every one of them dogs went in the wrong direction? No wonder it was so hard to find her. They misled the rescue squad. How can that many dogs be wrong?" a balding man asked, not seeking an answer.

Ginger's daddy emerged through the emergency room doors. "The doctors say she is going to be okay. No permanent damage is expected," he announced. A smile crossed his lips for the first time in two days. His broad grin beamed to match the beautiful day. Suddenly, a serious look replaced it as he spoke words from his heart.

"What an ordeal. Thank you all for being there. Somehow, it seems God was saying, 'Take your men, and take your all-terrain vehicles, and take your walkie-talkies, and your helicopter, and your dogs, and all you know about the effects of drugs. Take all your knowledge of the woods and all of your logic, and you will fail so that God can take your heart as His miraculous power is revealed to you.' "

There was a chorus of "Amen's" among the listeners. They knew with certainty that they had witnessed a miracle.

Today, Ginger is no longer haunted by depression. Like the preacher said, "God don't work no half miracles." Today, Ginger is happy, has a great job, and truly believes that God spared her life. She is more precious than ever to her mama and daddy, who know without a doubt that God still performs miracles.

Rest assured that this story is true and know that I will never be the same after that cold November day—the day God saved my daughter, Ginger Eades. You see, there really *was* a miracle on Boswell Road. Praise be to God!

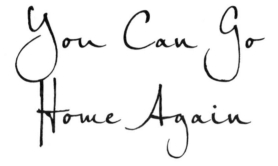

You Can Go Home Again

A few words from the author...

Thomas Wolfe was a great writer whose most famous quote contains the words "You can't go home again." "Sad but false words," is what I like to say about this quote. Perhaps I should explain exactly what I mean by this statement.

Throughout my book, I have alluded to the fact that I was glad Grandma Allen did not live to see what a mess I had made of my life. In 1993, I was working in Mississippi and began to play slot machines at the fancy new casinos. Within a year, I was totally out of control. I spiraled downward faster than a one-winged jet. When I crashed, I had seventeen high-limit credit cards maxed out and had lost everything I owned. I wasn't some high roller, just another gambling addict rolling around in the gutter of his addiction.

As a result of my addiction, my wonderful wife, Karen, attempted suicide to escape the unbelievable pain I had brought to her and our life together. The hospital pumped the pills from her stomach and she recovered, at least physically. It's hard to see the scars that we leave in a person's mind, but I am sure that they remained as I continued to gamble.

One night, a month before Karen's attempt, I had had my own brush with suicide. I had stopped at a highway rest area after losing whatever little money we had left. I reached into the glove compartment to get my pistol to end my life. Death seemed less painful than facing Karen once again with the awful news that I had been gambling. The pistol was gone. Karen had taken it out of the car, not to save my life but so she could sell it to get money to keep the utility company from turning off our electricity.

Two thwarted suicide attempts, absolutely penniless, spiritually and morally bankrupt, not to mention a Chapter 13 bankruptcy with a repayment schedule that took a huge chunk of whatever I made—and these were only a few of the consequences of my addiction. I had losses that could not be expressed in numbers.

I had lost my way and stopped attending church. I had lost my relationship with God; and Sundays would find me at the casino bowing down before the metal altar of the slot machine, where I would gamble until every last penny was gone. I had lost my self-respect and reputation while becoming a liar, a cheat, and a most sinful man. Although I tried several secular approaches to recover from my addiction, I continued to gamble.

Finally, I decided I could not recover living close to the casinos. We moved to Tennessee on borrowed money from a friend. However, the temptation moved with me, and I would drive six hours to Tunica to gamble whenever I could scrape up enough money to make the trip worth the drive. Karen and I were in the midst of this struggle with my addiction when Ginger came to live with us following her second suicide attempt in North Carolina. The rest of the *Miracle on Boswell Road* story you need to know is that I had been secretly squirreling away money, hiding it under the carpet in the trunk of the car. In fact, the weekend Ginger went off to end her life, I had planned on going gambling.

When God performed His miracle on Boswell Road, I underwent a profound change. When Karen and I returned home from the ICU on that Sunday night, I stood in the bright starlight, opened the trunk, and pulled out the money hidden under the carpet. I gave it to her, telling her we would need that money for hospital bills. Karen simply smiled, showing me the grace of God in her actions.

Christ said the prodigal son could come home. I had never forgotten this parable that Christ told to illustrate the love and forgiveness of our heavenly Father. That night I told God that I was terribly weary and confessed to Him all the wrong things I had done. I humbly asked Him to forgive me and let me come home to Him once again. Any pretense about who I was fell from me like leaves on a windy December day. There I was, broke and broken, down on my knees, knowing I was nothing but a lost sinner who had been living in the sty of gambling addiction for over three years. The truth is, I reeked from the stench of my behaviors and was repulsed by my own appearance. But, like Christ had said about the prodigal son, I had come to myself and was ready for the journey home no matter what lay in store for me.

That night, down on all fours, I asked God to take over my life and make me a new creature in Christ. I asked Him to transform me into a person I could stand to look at in the mirror. God is true to His word. I imagine I must have resembled a stray dog sitting at the screened-in back door of God's house, but I know for certain that that night He flung open the door and welcomed me home with open arms. I am a new creature.

God has transformed me. I am a changed man with a new mind and spirit.

Because of that miracle with Ginger, I have stopped gambling, and with God's guidance and help, have even written a Christ-centered gambling addiction recovery book. God has softened my heart once again and enabled me to write this book. With God, all things are truly possible. Christ is right. You can go home again! Hallelujah and Amen!

About the Author

JOHN M. EADES has a Ph.D. in counseling and has, in his twenty years of professional experience, come to the conclusion that a spiritual transformation must take place in order for the patient to have a successful recovery. As he observes individual's lives change as  they change spiritually, he has come to the realization that the majority of psychological miseries affecting his patients resulted from alienation from God.

John is a Christian, and an active member of his church. An award-winning author of short story collections, his previous publications include *The 7th Floor Ain't Too High for Angels to Fly* and *Waiting on Halley's Comet* (Health Communications, Inc.). John is a visiting professor at several universities, and conducts seminars on Drug and Alcohol Addiction, Gambling Addiction, and Human Motivation. He has written a book on gambling addiction based on his struggles and personal victory over gambling.

To order *Gambling Addiction: The Problem, the Pain, and the Pathway to Recovery*, send $10.95 c/o John Eades, 1355 Boswell Road, Winchester, TN 37398.

John and his wife, Karen, live in a country farmhouse in Winchester, Tennessee.